Treasure House

Teacher's Guide 5
Spelling Skills

Author: Sarah Snashall

William Collins' dream of knowledge for all began with the publication of his first book in 1819.

A self-educated mill worker, he not only enriched millions of lives, but also founded a flourishing publishing house. Today, staying true to this spirit, Collins books are packed with inspiration, innovation and practical expertise. They place you at the centre of a world of possibility and give you exactly what you need to explore it.

Collins. Freedom to teach.

Published by Collins
An imprint of HarperCollins*Publishers*
The News Building
1 London Bridge Street
London
SE1 9GF

Browse the complete Collins catalogue at
www.collins.co.uk

978-0-00-822312-0

British Library Cataloguing in Publication Data

A catalogue record for this publication is available from the British Library.

Publishing Director: Lee Newman
Publishing Manager: Helen Doran
Senior Editor: Hannah Dove
Project Manager: Emily Hooton
Author: Sarah Snashall
Development Editor: Jessica Marshall
Copy-editor: Karen Williams
Proofreader: Ros and Chris Davies
Cover design and artwork: Amparo Barrera and Ken Vail Graphic Design
Internal design concept: Amparo Barrera
Typesetter: Jouve India Private Ltd
Illustrations: Alberto Saichann (Beehive Illustration)
Production Controller: Rachel Weaver

Printed and bound by CPI Group (UK) Ltd, Croydon, CR0 4YY

Contents

About Treasure House

Treasure House is a comprehensive and flexible bank of books and online resources for teaching the English curriculum. The Treasure House series offers two different pathways: one covering each English strand discretely (Skills Focus Pathway) and one integrating texts and the strands to create a programme of study (Integrated English Pathway). This Teacher's Guide is part of the Skills Focus Pathway.

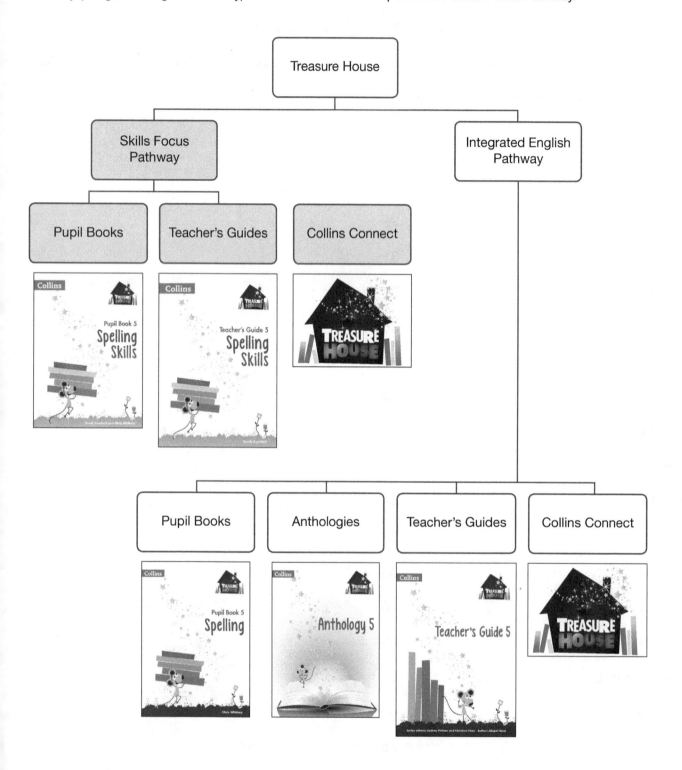

1. Skills Focus

The Skills Focus Pupil Books and Teacher's Guides for all four strands (Comprehension; Spelling; Composition; and Vocabulary, Grammar and Punctuation) allow you to teach each curriculum area in a targeted way. Each unit in the Pupil Book is mapped directly to the statutory requirements of the National Curriculum. Each Teacher's Guide provides step-by-step instructions to guide you through the Pupil Book activities and digital Collins Connect resources for each competency. With a clear focus on skills and clearly-listed curriculum objectives you can select the appropriate resources to support your lessons.

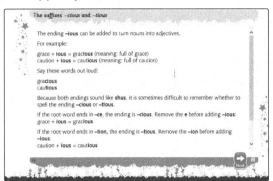

2. Integrated English

Alternatively, the Integrated English pathway offers a complete programme of genre-based teaching sequences. There is one Teacher's Guide and one Anthology for each year group. Each Teacher's Guide provides 15 teaching sequences focused on different genres of text such as fairy tales, letters and newspaper articles. The Anthologies contain the classic texts, fiction, non-fiction and poetry required for each sequence. Each sequence also weaves together all four dimensions of the National Curriculum for English – Comprehension; Spelling; Composition; and Vocabulary, Grammar and Punctuation – into a complete English programme. The Pupil Books and Collins Connect provide targeted explanation of key points and practice activities organised by strand. This programme provides 30 weeks of teaching inspiration.

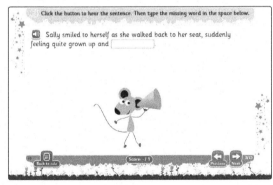

Other components

Handwriting Books, Handwriting Workbooks, Word Books and the online digital resources on Collins Connect are suitable for use with both pathways.

Treasure House Skills Focus Teacher's Guides

Year	Comprehension	Composition	Vocabulary, Grammar and Punctuation	Spelling
1	978-0-00-822290-1	978-0-00-822302-1	978-0-00-822296-3	978-0-00-822308-3
2	978-0-00-822291-8	978-0-00-822303-8	978-0-00-822297-0	978-0-00-822309-0
3	978-0-00-822292-5	978-0-00-822304-5	978-0-00-822298-7	978-0-00-822310-6
4	978-0-00-822293-2	978-0-00-822305-2	978-0-00-822299-4	978-0-00-822311-3
5	978-0-00-822294-9	978-0-00-822306-9	978-0-00-822300-7	978-0-00-822312-0
6	978-0-00-822295-6	978-0-00-822307-6	978-0-00-822301-4	978-0-00-822313-7

Inside the Skills Focus Teacher's Guides

The teaching notes in each unit of the Teacher's Guide provide you with subject information or background, a range of whole class and differentiated activities including photocopiable resource sheets and links to the Pupil Book and the online Collins Connect activities.

Each **Overview** provides clear objectives for each lesson tied into the new curriculum, links to the other relevant components and a list of any additional resources required.

Teaching overview introduces each spelling rule and provides a list of key words that follow the rule that are useful to the age group.

Support, embed & challenge supports a mastery approach with activities provided at three levels.

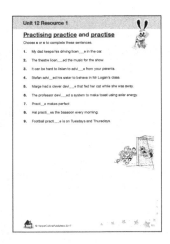

Pupil practice gives guidance and the answers to each of the three sections in the Pupil Book: *Get started*, *Try these* and *Now try these*.

Introduce the concept provides 5–10 minutes of preliminary discussion points or class/group activities to get the pupils engaged in the lesson focus and set out any essential prior learning.

Homework / Additional activities lists ideas for classroom or homework activities, and relevant activities from Collins Connect.

Two photocopiable **resource** worksheets per unit provide extra practice of the specific lesson concept. They are designed to be used with the activities in support, embed or challenge sections.

Treasure House Skills Focus Pupil Books

There are four Skills Focus Pupil Books for each year group, based on the four dimensions of the National Curriculum for English: Comprehension; Spelling; Composition; and Vocabulary, Grammar and Punctuation. The Pupil Books provide a child-friendly introduction to each subject and a range of initial activities for independent pupil-led learning. A Review unit for each term assesses pupils' progress.

Year	Comprehension	Composition	Vocabulary, Grammar and Punctuation	Spelling
1	978-0-00-823634-2	978-0-00-823646-5	978-0-00-823640-3	978-0-00-823652-6
2	978-0-00-823635-9	978-0-00-823647-2	978-0-00-823641-0	978-0-00-823653-3
3	978-0-00-823636-6	978-0-00-823648-9	978-0-00-823642-7	978-0-00-823654-0
4	978-0-00-823637-3	978-0-00-823649-6	978-0-00-823643-4	978-0-00-823655-7
5	978-0-00-823638-0	978-0-00-823650-2	978-0-00-823644-1	978-0-00-823656-4
6	978-0-00-823639-7	978-0-00-823651-9	978-0-00-823645-8	978-0-00-823657-1

Inside the Skills Focus Pupil Books

Comprehension

Includes high-quality text extracts covering poetry, prose, traditional tales, playscripts and non-fiction.

Pupils retrieve and record information, learn to draw inferences from texts and increase their familiarity with a wide range of literary genres.

Composition

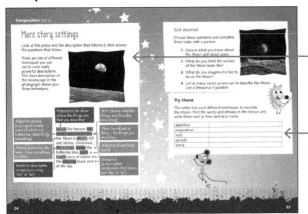

Includes high-quality, annotated text extracts as models for different types of writing.

Children learn how to write effectively and for a purpose.

Vocabulary, Grammar and Punctuation

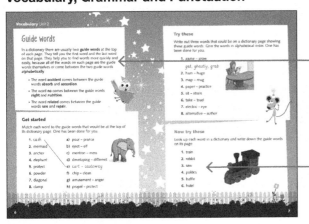

Develops children's knowledge and understanding of grammar and punctuation skills.

A rule is introduced and explained. Children are given lots of opportunities to practise using it.

Spelling

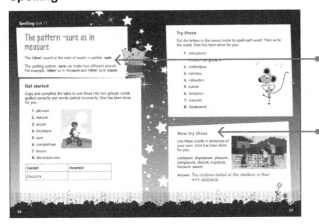

Spelling rules are introduced and explained.

Practice is provided for spotting and using the spelling rules, correcting misspelt words and using the words in context.

Treasure House on Collins Connect

Digital resources for Treasure House are available on Collins Connect which provides a wealth of interactive activities. Treasure House is organised into six core areas on Collins Connect:

- Comprehension
- Spelling
- Composition
- Vocabulary, Grammar and Punctuation
- The Reading Attic
- Teacher's Guides and Anthologies.

For most units in the Skills Focus Pupil Books, there is an accompanying Collins Connect unit focused on the same teaching objective. These fun, independent activities can be used for initial pupil-led learning, or for further practice using a different learning environment. Either way, with Collins Connect, you have a wealth of questions to help children embed their learning.

Treasure House on Collins Connect is available via subscription at connect.collins.co.uk

Features of Treasure House on Collins Connect

The digital resources enhance children's comprehension, spelling, composition, and vocabulary, grammar, punctuation skills through providing:

- a bank of varied and engaging interactive activities so children can practise their skills independently
- audio support to help children access the texts and activities
- auto-mark functionality so children receive instant feedback and have the opportunity to repeat tasks.

Teachers benefit from useful resources and time-saving tools including:

- teacher-facing materials such as audio and explanations for front-of-class teaching or pupil-led learning
- lesson starter videos for some Composition units
- downloadable teaching notes for all online activities
- downloadable teaching notes for Skills Focus and Integrated English pathways
- the option to assign homework activities to your classes
- class records to monitor progress.

Comprehension

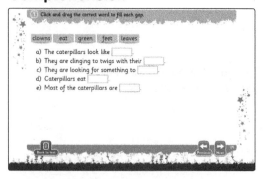

- Includes high-quality text extracts covering poetry, prose, traditional tales, playscripts and non-fiction.
- Audio function supports children to access the text and the activities

Composition

- Activities support children to develop and build more sophisticated sentence structures.
- Every unit ends with a longer piece of writing that can be submitted to the teacher for marking.

Vocabulary, Grammar and Punctuation

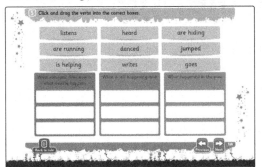

- Fun, practical activities develop children's knowledge and understanding of grammar and punctuation skills.
- Each skill is reinforced with a huge, varied bank of practice questions.

Spelling

- Fun, practical activities develop children's knowledge and understanding of each spelling rule.
- Each rule is reinforced with a huge, varied bank of practice questions.
- Children spell words using an audio prompt, write their own sentences and practise spelling using Look Say Cover Write Check.

Reading Attic

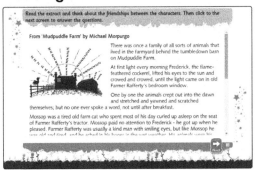

- Children's love of reading is nurtured with texts from exciting children's authors including Micheal Bond, David Walliams and Micheal Morpurgo.
- Lesson sequences accompany the texts, with drama opportunities and creative strategies for engaging children with key themes, characters and plots.
- Whole-book projects encourage reading for pleasure.

Treasure House Digital Teacher's Guides and Anthologies

The teaching sequences and anthology texts for each year group are included as a flexible bank of resources.

The teaching notes for each skill strand and year group are also included on Collins Connect.

Support, embed and challenge

Treasure House provides comprehensive, detailed differentiation at three levels to ensure that all children are able to access achievement. It is important that children master the basic skills before they go further in their learning. Children may make progress towards the standard at different speeds, with some not reaching it until the very end of the year.

In the Teacher's Guide, Support, Embed and Challenge sections allow teachers to keep the whole class focussed with no child left behind. Two photocopiable resources per unit offer additional material linked to the Support, Embed or Challenge sections.

Support

The Support section in Spelling offers scaffolded activities (suitable for use in small groups with adult support) that will help learners who have not yet grasped the specific spelling rule. These activities use fewer or more straightforward words and are usually supported with a photocopiable resource sheet.

If you have a teaching assistant, you may wish to ask him or her to help children work through these activities. You might then ask children who have completed these activities to progress to other more challenging tasks found in the Embed or Challenge sections – or you may decide more practice of the basics is required. Collins Connect can provide further activities.

Embed

The Embed section includes activities to embed learning and is aimed at those who children who are working at the expected standard. It ensures that learners have understood key teaching objectives for the age-group. These activities could be used by the whole class or groups, and most are appropriate for both teacher-led and independent work.

In Spelling, the Embed section provides activities to embed learning following the whole class introduction and is aimed at those who children who are working at the expected standard. After the children have learnt each rule, this section provides a range of fun small group games and activities to help the children (working without an adult) to learn words with the spelling pattern. A photocopiable resource sheet is provided for each unit.

Challenge

The Challenge section provides additional tasks, questions or activities that will push children who have mastered the spelling rule without difficulty. This keeps children motivated and allows them to gain a greater depth of understanding. You may wish to give these activities to fast finishers to work through independently.

Children who are working above the expected level may progress to focusing on the spelling of less common, longer words or they might investigate exceptions to the rule and creating posters for the class. Challenge activities are provided to stretch the children's understanding of the rule or to enhance vocabulary work.

Differentiated spelling lists

In the Homework section, you will find word lists for spelling tests. There is a standard list and there are also two targeted lists; *Support words* list is suitable for children who are struggling with the concept. The list is shorter and contains words that are more common, shorter, simpler or more regular. The *Challenge words* list is a longer list often with more challenging words, suitable for children who have grasped the rule/concept.

Differentiated weekly spelling lists are provided for each unit and details of any matching Collins Connect units.

Assessment

Teacher's Guide

There are opportunities for assessment throughout the Treasure House series. The teaching notes in the Skills Focus Teacher's Guides offer ideas for questions, informal assessment and spelling tests.

Pupil Book Review units

Each Pupil Book has three Review units designed as a quick formative assessment tool for the end of each term. Questions assess the work that has been covered over the previous units. These review units will provide you with an informal way of measuring your pupils' progress. You may wish to use these as Assessment *for* Learning to help you and your pupils to understand where they are in their learning journey.

The Review units in the Spelling and Vocabulary, Grammar and Punctuation Pupil Books, include questions testing rules taught in preceding units. By mixing questions on different unit topics within exercises, children can show understanding of multiple rules and patterns.

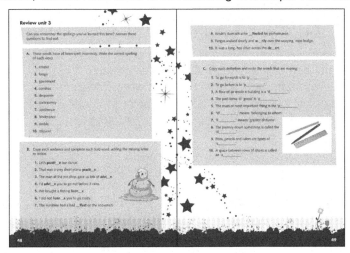

Assessment in Collins Connect

Activities on Collins Connect can also be used for effective assessment. Activities with auto-marking mean that if children answer incorrectly, they can make another attempt helping them to analyse their own work for mistakes. Homework activities can also be assigned to classes through Collins Connect. At the end of activities, children can select a smiley face to indicate how they found the task giving you useful feedback on any gaps in knowledge.

Class records on Collins Connect allow you to get an overview of children's progress with several features. You can choose to view records by unit, pupil or strand. By viewing detailed scores, you can view pupils' scores question by question in a clear table-format to help you establish areas where there might be particular strengths and weaknesses both class-wide and for individuals.

If you wish, you can also set mastery judgements (mastery achieved and exceeded, mastery achieved, mastery not yet achieved) to help see where your children need more help.

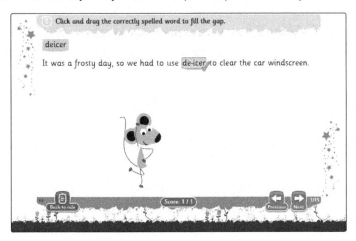

Support with teaching spelling

Trying to teach and understand the vagaries of English spelling is enough to drive the most patient of us to distraction. Think on those lucky countries such as Poland with phonetically consistent spelling. However, many words in English are phonetic and this should remain our starting point for all unknown words, with the children becoming increasingly confident in their knowledge of the spelling options for each sound.

The National Curriculum in England encourages us to teach the rules and patterns that are associated with each spelling cluster. In some cases these rules are easy to absorb, for example 'i before c except after c'. Others remain more elusive, such as hearing the stress in a word before deciding whether to double the last letter or not. You will have to judge for yourself when the rule is going to aid children in their learning and when they would be better off just learning the rules. (There are times when you have just got your head around a complicated rule to discover that there are only five suitable words for your class.) However, a knowledge and understanding of rules that do apply will provide children with the skills to manipulate language and root words, such as by adding suffixes and prefixes, to create specific vocabulary for their writing. This in turn will increase their confidence in writing. Teaching children to understand the relationship between words, such as 'grace' and 'gracious' not only develops their vocabulary but aids their spelling too.

This spelling scheme by its nature focuses on learning words as a separate activity: games, spelling tests and sometimes sentences. But, of course, this is only part of the picture. Children who read a lot will naturally absorb spelling as they regularly come across common words. Children who write a lot will naturally practise words that they want to use. Learning to spell words is only of any use if you use them at some point. Therefore, the activities in this scheme can only form part of the picture.

Weekly spelling test

The weekly spelling test remains crucial to learning the huge bank of words needed by the end of primary school. Spelling lists are provided in this scheme, but you may want to add or remove words depending on the abilities of the children in your class and the number of words you feel it is appropriate for them to learn. You will need to strike a balance between developing their vocabulary and providing useful words for them to learn.

You may also wish to enhance their spelling lists with words that they have spelt wrong during their writing tasks, or specific topic-led vocabulary.

Spelling games

The activities in this scheme aim to be fun and game-like. Many of the activities in the book are introduced for use with a particular set of words but many can be adapted for any word list you are practising (they mainly involve creating a set of word cards):

Pairs: Create two sets of word cards for the words you are practising and use them to play a game of pairs. Alternatively, use words with and without suffixes and prefixes or words related in other ways (such as different spellings for the same sound or homophones) and challenge the children to find the two associated words.

Simon's Game: When asking the children to learn a specific set of words, such as words with 'c' for /s/, ask pairs of children to remember the words on the list.

Pick a card: the children place a set of word cards between them and take turns to draw a card and test their partner or the next child around the table.

Hangman: Tell the children to play Hangman using words from previous two or three weeks' spellings. This encourages an attention to the specific letters and can be particularly useful when practising words with silent letters.

Bingo: Create Bingo cards for the words you are studying (ensuring each card has a slightly different word selection). When playing Bingo, the children spend the session staring at the words on their sheet – a useful way to add the word to the subconscious.

Game board: Create a simple board game where the children roll a dice to progress along a series of squares some of which require them to spell one of the words from the list (when someone draws a card and reads it to them). The board can be reused with any new set of words cards.

Differentiation

The lesson plans in this book provide three levels of differentiation. However, you may wish to provide further practice (Support or Challenge) at Years 3 and 4 or Years 5 and 6 by supplying the relevant children with the book for the other year group, as the words covered are the same. You may also wish to recap on words from earlier years for those children whose spelling needs further help.

48. accommodate	49. occur	50. immediately	**Finish**
47. correspond	46. attached	45. committee	44. exaggerate
40. suggest	41. recommend	42. occupy	43. programme
39. necessary	38. profession	37. immediate	36. apparent
32. interrupt	33. opportunity	34. excellent	35. embarrass
31. marvellous	30. soldier	29. thorough	28. stomach
24. parliament	25. persuade	26. restaurant	27. shoulder
23. mischievous	22. privilege	21. queue	20. neighbour
16. muscle	17. leisure	18. definite	19. nuisance
15. bargain	14. category	13. disastrous	12. yacht
8. sincerely	9. vehicle	10. vegetable	11. bruise
7. signature	6. awkward	5. forty	4. lightning
Start	1. twelfth	2. variety	3. physical

m	u	s	c	l	e	q	g	g	a	s
a	j	b	w	e	q	g	o	h	j	e
w	d	e	f	i	n	i	t	e	d	c
h	v	h	m	s	x	m	a	z	y	r
c	e	x	n	u	i	s	a	n	c	e
m	f	b	g	r	s	o	n	b	m	t
q	u	e	u	e	h	l	k	p	z	a
y	o	y	g	o	c	d	s	z	e	r
j	s	d	k	f	l	i	f	v	n	y
p	r	i	v	i	l	e	g	e	k	n
x	d	f	k	r	y	r	v	m	c	k
n	e	i	g	h	b	o	u	r	v	e

Delivering the 2014 National Curriculum for English

Unit	Title	Treasure House resources	Collins Connect	English Programme of Study	KS2 English Grammar, Punctuation and Spelling Test code
1	The suffixes –cious and –tious	• Spelling Skills Pupil Book 5, Unit 1, pages 4–5 • Spelling Skills Teacher's Guide 5 – Unit 1, pages 22–24 – Photocopiable Unit 1, Resource 1: Ambitious adjectives, page 76 – Photocopiable Unit 1, Resource 2: Don't be anxious about spelling, page 77	Treasure House Spelling Year 5, Unit 1	Endings which sound like /ʃəs/ spelt –cious or –tious	S53
2	The suffixes –cial and –tial	• Spelling Skills Pupil Book 5, Unit 2, pages 6–7 • Spelling Skills Teacher's Guide 5 – Unit 2, pages 25–27 – Photocopiable Unit 2, Resource 1: An unofficial outing, page 78 – Photocopiable Unit 2, Resource 2: Essential words, beneficial spellings, page 79	Treasure House Spelling Year 5, Unit 2	Endings which sound like /ʃəl/	S54
3A	The suffixes –ant and –ent	• Spelling Skills Pupil Book 5, Unit 3A, pages 8–9 • Spelling Skills Teacher's Guide 5 – Unit 3A, pages 28–30 – Photocopiable Unit 3A, Resource 1: Important spellings for intelligent students, page 80 – Photocopiable Unit 3A, Resource 2: Relevant words, significant sentences, page 81	Treasure House Spelling Year 5, Unit 3	Words ending in –ant, –ance/–ancy, –ent, –ence/–ency	S55

Unit	Title	Treasure House resources	Collins Connect	English Programme of Study	KS2 English Grammar, Punctuation and Spelling Test code

3B	The suffixes –ence, –ency, –ance and –ancy	• Spelling Skills Pupil Book 5, Unit 3B, pages 10–11
		• Spelling Skills Teacher's Guide 5
		  – Unit 3B, pages 31–33
		  – Photocopiable Unit 3B, Resource 1: Spell with confid<u>ence</u>, page 82
		  – Photocopiable Unit 3B, Resource 2: Spell with compet<u>ency</u>, page 83
				Words ending in –ant, –ance/–ancy, –ent, –ence/–ency	S55

3C	Common words (1)	• Spelling Skills Pupil Book 5, Unit 3C, pages 12–13
		• Spelling Skills Teacher's Guide 5
		  – Unit 3C, pages 34–35
		  – Photocopiable Unit 3C, Resource 1: Appreciate these excellent words! page 84
		  – Photocopiable Unit 3C, Resource 2: Excellent words to communicate with, page 85
				Word list – years 5 and 6	S37

4	The suffixes –able, –ible, –ably and –ibly	• Spelling Skills Pupil Book 5, Unit 4, pages 14–15
		• Spelling Skills Teacher's Guide 5
		  – Unit 4, pages 36–38
		  – Photocopiable Unit 4, Resource 1: Are you <u>able</u> to add <u>ible</u> and <u>able</u>? page 86
		  – Photocopiable Unit 4, Resource 2: Sen<u>sible</u> words spelt predicta<u>bly</u>, page 87
			Treasure House Spelling Year 5, Unit 4	Words ending in –able and –ible
				Words ending in –ably and –ibly
					S56

5	Adding suffixes beginning with vowels to words ending in –fer	• Spelling Skills Pupil Book 5, Unit 5, pages 16–17
		• Spelling Skills Teacher's Guide 5
		  – Unit 5, pages 39–41
		  – Photocopiable Unit 5, Resource 1: <u>Suffering</u> from stress, page 88
		  – Photocopiable Unit 5, Resource 2: Can you hear the <u>difference</u>? page 89
			Treasure House Spelling Year 5, Unit 5	Adding suffixes beginning with vowel letters to words ending in –fer	S57

Unit	Title	Treasure House resources	Collins Connect	English Programme of Study	KS2 English Grammar, Punctuation and Spelling Test code
6A	Common words (2)	• Spelling Skills Pupil Book 5, Unit 6A, pages 20–21 • Spelling Skills Teacher's Guide 5 – Unit 6A, pages 43–44 – Photocopiable Unit 6A, Resource 1: Marvellous words to occupy you, page 90 – Photocopiable Unit 6A, Resource 2: An opportunity to learn necessary spellings, page 91		Word list – years 5 and 6	S37
6B	Use of the hyphen after prefixes	• Spelling Skills Pupil Book 5, Unit 6B, pages 22–23 • Spelling Skills Teacher's Guide 5 – Unit 6B, pages 45–47 – Photocopiable Unit 6B, Resource 1: Re-examining hyphens, page 92 – Photocopiable Unit 6B, Resource 2: Re-enforcing good hyphenation, page 93	Treasure House Spelling Year 5, Unit 6	Use of the hyphen	G6.13
7A	The /ee/ sound spelt ei after c	• Spelling Skills Pupil Book 5, Unit 7A, pages 24–25 • Spelling Skills Teacher's Guide 5 – Unit 7A, pages 48–50 – Photocopiable Unit 7A, Resource 1: Seize the ei spelling! page 94 – Photocopiable Unit 7A, Resource 2: Let neither /ee/ spelling give you grief, page 95	Treasure House Spelling Year 5, Unit 7	Words with the /i:/ sound spelt ei after c	S58
7B	Common words (3)	• Spelling Skills Pupil Book 5, Unit 7B, pages 26–27 • Spelling Skills Teacher's Guide 5 – Unit 7B, pages 51–52 – Photocopiable Unit 7B, Resource 1: Mischievous spellings word search, page 96 – Photocopiable Unit 7B, Resource 2: Spelling nuisance words, page 97		Word list – years 5 and 6	S37

Unit	Title	Treasure House resources	Collins Connect	English Programme of Study	KS2 English Grammar, Punctuation and Spelling Test code

8	The letter-string ough	• Spelling Skills Pupil Book 5, Unit 8, pages 28–29
		• Spelling Skills Teacher's Guide 5
		  – Unit 8, pages 53–55
		  – Photocopiable Unit 8, Resource 1: Enough tough spellings! page 98
		  – Photocopiable Unit 8, Resource 2: Thoroughly tough words, page 99
				Words containing the letter-string ough	S59

9A	Words with 'silent' letters	• Spelling Skills Pupil Book 5, Unit 9A, pages 30–31
		• Spelling Skills Teacher's Guide 5
		  – Unit 9A, pages 56–58
		  – Photocopiable Unit 9A, Resource 1: Sorting 'silent' letters, page 100
		  – Photocopiable Unit 9A, Resource 2: Subtle spellings, page 101
			Treasure House Spelling Year 5, Unit 9	Words with 'silent' letters (i.e. letters whose presence cannot be predicted from the pronunciation of the word)	S60

9B	Common words (4)	• Spelling Skills Pupil Book 5, Unit 9B, pages 32–33
		• Spelling Skills Teacher's Guide 5
		  – Unit 9B, pages 59–60
		  – Photocopiable Unit 9B, Resource 1: Lightning crossword, page 102
		  – Photocopiable Unit 9B, Resource 2: Disastrous Snakes and Ladders, pages 103–104
				Word list – years 5 and 6	S37

10A	Common words (5)	• Spelling Skills Pupil Book 5, Unit 10A, pages 36–37
		• Spelling Skills Teacher's Guide 5
		  – Unit 10A, pages 62–64
		  – Photocopiable Unit 10A, Resource 1: A 'conscious' or 'conscience' controversy, page 105
		  – Photocopiable Unit 10A, Resource 2: Playing with words, page 106
				Word list – Years 5 and 6	S37

Unit	Title	Treasure House resources	Collins Connect	English Programme of Study	KS2 English Grammar, Punctuation and Spelling Test code

10B	Homophones and near-homophones (1)	• Spelling Skills Pupil Book 5, Unit 10B, pages 38–39
		• Spelling Skills Teacher's Guide 5
		  – Unit 10B, pages 65–66
		  – Photocopiable Unit 10B, Resource 1: Are you <u>weary</u> of spelling mistakes? page 107
		  – Photocopiable Unit 10B, Resource 2: <u>Proceed</u> to spell <u>effectively</u>, page 108
			Treasure House Spelling Year 5, Unit 10	Homophones and other words that are often confused	S61

11	Homophones and near-homophones (2)	• Spelling Skills Pupil Book 5, Unit 11, pages 40–41
		• Spelling Skills Teacher's Guide 5
		  – Unit 11, pages 67–68
		  – Photocopiable Unit 11, Resource 1: Put spelling errors in the <u>past</u>, page 109
		  – Photocopiable Unit 11, Resource 2: A full <u>complement</u> of homophones, page 110
			Treasure House Spelling Year 5, Unit 11	Homophones and other words that are often confused	S61

12	Homophones and near-homophones (3)	• Spelling Skills Pupil Book 5, Unit 12, pages 42–43
		• Spelling Skills Teacher's Guide 5
		  – Unit 12, pages 69–70
		  – Photocopiable Unit 12, Resource 1: <u>Practising</u> practice and <u>practise</u>, page 111
		  – Photocopiable Unit 12, Resource 2: Higher homophones, page 112
			Treasure House Spelling Year 5, Unit 12	Homophones and other words that are often confused	S61

13	Homophones and near-homophones (4)	• Spelling Skills Pupil Book 5, Unit 13, pages 44–45
		• Spelling Skills Teacher's Guide 5
		  – Unit 13, pages 71–72
		  – Photocopiable Unit 13, Resource 1: Homophone crossword, page 113
		  – Photocopiable Unit 13, Resource 2: A short <u>course</u> in more homophones, page 114
			Treasure House Spelling Year 5, Unit 13	Homophones and other words that are often confused	S61

Unit	Title	Treasure House resources	Collins Connect	English Programme of Study	KS2 English Grammar, Punctuation and Spelling Test code
14	Homophones and near-homophones (5)	• Spelling Skills Pupil Book 5, Unit 14, pages 46–47 • Spelling Skills Teacher's Guide 5 – Unit 14, pages 73–74 – Photocopiable Unit 14, Resource 1: Who's decent at spelling? page 115 – Photocopiable Unit 14, Resource 2: Homophones: There's meaning at stake, page 116	Treasure House Spelling Year 5, Unit 14	Homophones and other words that are often confused	S61

Unit 1: The suffixes –cious and –tious

Overview

English curriculum objectives

- Endings which sound like /shus/ spelt –cious and –tious

Treasure House resources

- Spelling Skills Pupil Book 5, Unit 1, pages 4–5
- Collins Connect Treasure House Spelling Year 5, Unit 1
- Photocopiable Unit 1, Resource 1: Amb<u>itious</u> adjectives, page 76

- Photocopiable Unit 1, Resource 2: Don't be anx<u>ious</u> about spelling, page 77

Additional resources

- Word cards: spacious, gracious, delicious, ferocious, vicious, luscious, atrocious, unconscious, cautious, infectious, nutritious, ambitious, superstitious, pretentious, malicious, scrumptious, anxious
- A bag to draw word cards from

Introduction

Teaching overview

Many of the examples in this unit are challenging, but you should encourage the children to be ambitious about using them. The endings '–cious' and '–tious' both spell /shus/ and children must learn to choose the correct ending. Some root nouns provide a clue: the '–cious' ending is used with root words ending '–ce' (the 'e' must be removed before adding 'ious') and the '–tious' ending is used with root words ending '–tion' (remove 'tion' and add 'tious').
Of course, there are many words ending '–cious' and '–tious' that have root words with a different pattern, for example, 'ferocity' → 'ferocious', 'delicacy' → 'delicious'. Others have no obvious root, such as 'conscious'. These just have to be learned.

Introduce the concept

Organise the children into groups. Give each group a set of word cards (see Additional resources). Ask them to try reading the words. Ask for someone to volunteer a word and write it on the board.

Underline 'cious' or 'tious' and establish that this cluster of letters spells /shus/. Provide more time for the children to read the word cards. Ask for more volunteers to give you words and tell you which letters to underline for the /shus/ sound. Tell the groups to sort their words into those they know the meanings of and those they do not. Ask each group which words they did not understand and clarify the meanings of those words for them.

Write the words 'spacious', 'gracious', 'delicious', 'ferocious', 'vicious', 'atrocious', 'cautious', 'infectious', 'nutritious', 'ambitious', 'superstitious', 'pretentious' and 'malicious' on the board. Introduce the associated nouns: 'space', 'grace', 'delicacy', 'ferocity', 'vice', 'atrocity', 'caution', 'infection', 'nutrition', 'ambition', 'superstition', 'pretention' and 'malice'. Show how these nouns can be converted into the adjectives.

Explain that 'anxious' related to the noun 'anxiety' has its own spelling of /shus/ that needs to be learned.

Pupil practice

Pupil Book pages 4–5

Get started

In this activity, children copy and complete a table, sorting words into two groups: words ending '–cious' and words ending '–tious'. Ask the children to read each word and identify the /shus/ ending. Discuss the meaning of each word as many of them are difficult for Year 5 children.

Answers

Words ending '–cious'		Words ending '–tious'	
precious	[1 mark]	*scrumptious*	*[example]*
conscious	[1 mark]	cautious	[1 mark]
delicious	[1 mark]	ambitious	[1 mark]
ferocious	[1 mark]	fictitious	[1 mark]
		unambitious	[1 mark]
		incautious	[1 mark]

Try these

In this activity, children add '–cious' or '–tious' to words. Recap with the children on the rules of adding these endings. Read and explain the meanings of the root words. Say what each new word will be so the children know what to aim for. Discuss the meanings of the new words.

Answers

1. *vicious*		[example]
2. ambitious		[1 mark]
3. malicious		[1 mark]
4. spacious		[1 mark]
5. infectious		[1 mark]
6. nutritious		[1 mark]
7. superstitious		[1 mark]
8. pretentious		[1 mark]
9. gracious		[1 mark]
10. contentious		[1 mark]

Now try these

In this activity, children compose sentences for the target words 'ferocious', 'fictitious', 'anxious', 'cautious', 'unambitious', 'scrumptious', 'precious', 'unconscious', 'delicious' and 'incautious'. Read the words together and ensure that the children understand the meaning of each word, particularly 'unconscious' and 'incautious' (the opposite of 'cautious'). Tell the children to share their ideas with a partner before writing. Afterwards, share the children's sentences.

Suggested answers

Beneath the waves lurks a ferocious monster.

[example]

Accept any sentences where the target word is correctly spelt and used.
[10 marks: 1 mark per sentence]

Support, embed & challenge

Support

Ask these children to help you read through the word cards (see Additional resources) and underline the endings. Sort the words (except 'anxious') according to their endings: '–cious' or '–tious'. Put all the word cards in a bag. Ask the children to take turns to draw a card, read the word, say what the ending is and (with support) create a noun phrase for the word. Cut off the endings and muddle up the word parts. Take a root and ask the children help you decide what the ending should be, either by using their knowledge of the word or by thinking of the related noun.

Ask the children to complete Unit 1 Resource 1: Amb<u>itious</u> adjectives. (**Answers** space, spacious; grace, gracious; infection, infectious; nutrition, nutritious; ambition, ambitious; vice, vicious; anxiety, anxious; ferocity, ferocious; caution, cautious; delicacy, delicious) Afterwards, discuss the pairs of nouns and adjectives. Ask: 'Which nouns are helpful when spelling the related adjective?'

Embed

Organise the children into groups of three. Provide the groups with sets of word cards (see Additional resources). Ask them to sort the words into the three endings, '–cious', '–tious' and '–xious', and learn the words in each set. Challenge the children to remember some of the nouns related to these words. To help them associate words with the same spelling pattern, ask them to make up sentences using words with the same endings, for example: 'I was cautious about visiting Toby because he had an infectious disease so I made up a fictitious excuse.' 'The doughnut was not nutritious but it was scrumptious.' 'The precious jewel was guarded by a ferocious dragon.'

Ask the children to complete Unit 1 Resource 2: Don't be anx<u>ious</u> about spelling. (**Answers** 1. spacious, 2. nutritious, 3. precious, 4. ferocious, 5. cautious, 6. infectious, 7. anxious, 8. delicious; 1. anxious, 2. nutritious, 3. ferocious, 4. delicious, 5. cautious, 6. infectious, 7. precious, 8. spacious)

Challenge

There are many luscious and propitious adjectives with these endings. Ask these children to learn the meanings of the words 'pernicious', 'capricious', 'audacious', 'vexatious', 'ostentatious' and 'fractious'. Ask them to write a noun phrase for each word and then share their phrases with the class. Challenge them to use one of these words in their writing at some point in the week.

Homework / Additional activities

Spelling test

Ask the children to learn one of the following lists of words for a spelling test. Challenge them to write sentences for five of the words on their list.

Core words	Support words	Challenge words
spacious	spacious	spacious
gracious	gracious	gracious
delicious	delicious	delicious
ferocious	ferocious	ferocious
vicious	vicious	vicious
luscious	unconscious	luscious
atrocious	cautious	atrocious
unconscious	infectious	unconscious
cautious	nutritious	cautious
infectious	ambitious	infectious
nutritious		nutritious
ambitious		ambitious
superstitious		superstitious
pretentious		pretentious
		malicious
		scrumptious

Collins Connect: Unit 1

Ask the children to complete Unit 1 (see Teach → Year 5 → Spelling → Unit 1).

Unit 2: The suffixes –cial and –tial

Overview

English curriculum objectives

- Endings which sound like /shul/

Treasure House resources

- Spelling Skills Pupil Book 5, Unit 2, pages 6–7
- Collins Connect Treasure House Spelling Year 5, Unit 2
- Photocopiable Unit 2, Resource 1: An unofficial outing, page 78

- Photocopiable Unit 2, Resource 2: Essential words, beneficial spellings, page 79

Additional resources

- Word cards: antisocial, artificial, beneficial, confidential, commercial, crucial, facial, financial, glacial, influential, initial, insubstantial, judicial, martial, official, partial, potential, preferential, presidential, quintessential, racial, residential, sequential, social, special, substantial, superficial, torrential, unofficial

Introduction

Teaching overview

Words that end '–cial' and '–tial' are adjectives that end with the /shul/ sound. Although this rule is not foolproof, most words that end '–cial' have a vowel before the ending, for example, 'special' and 'official'; most words that end '–tial' have a consonant before the ending, for example, 'influential' and 'martial'. Exceptions to this rule are: 'financial', 'commercial', 'provincial' and 'initial'.

Introduce the concept

Hand out a word card to each child (see Additional resources). Ask them to read their word and discuss its meaning and spelling with a partner. Ask the children to put their hands up if their word ends in a /shul/ sound. Share some of the words, writing these on the board and underlining the endings. Organise

the children into groups and ask them to share their words. Tell them to sort their words into '–cial' and '–tial' endings. Ask them to shuffle the words again and sort them into words that have a vowel before the '–cial' or '–tial' ending and words that have a consonant before the '–cial' or '–tial' ending. Ask: 'Can you see a pattern?' Agree that, most commonly, '–cial' follows a vowel and '–tial' follows a consonant.

Point out the key exceptions: 'financial', 'commercial', 'provincial' and 'initial'.

Ask the children to work in their groups to create a noun phrase for one or two of their words, for example: 'an artificial leg', 'torrential rain', 'social worker'. Share the groups' ideas as a class. Establish that these words are all adjectives.

Pupil practice

Pupil Book pages 6–7

Get started

In this activity, children sort words into two groups: words ending '–cial' and words ending '–tial'. Afterwards, ask them to learn the words in each list.

Ask the children to write '–cial' on one side of their whiteboards and '–tial' on the other. Tell them to hide their answers to this activity. Read out the words and ask the children to hold up the appropriate ending for each word.

Answers

Words ending '–cial'		Words ending '–tial'	
financial	[1 mark]	*torrential*	*[example]*
special	[1 mark]	partial	[1 mark]
artificial	[1 mark]	initial	[1 mark]
provincial	[1 mark]		
social	[1 mark]		
commercial	[1 mark]		
unofficial	[1 mark]		

Try these

In this activity, children choose the correct endings for words. Remind them that –'cial' usually follows a vowel and '–tial' usually follows a consonant.

Answers

1. *facial*	[example]
2. residential	[1 mark]
3. circumstantial	[1 mark]
4. glacial	[1 mark]
5. insubstantial	[1 mark]
6. superficial	[1 mark]
7. potential	[1 mark]
8. crucial	[1 mark]
9. racial	[1 mark]
10. martial	[1 mark]

Now try these

In this activity, children copy and complete the sentences by choosing the correct spelling of each missing word. Read the sentences together and ensure that the children understand the words they are being asked to spell. To help them decide which ending to use, encourage the children to remember that '–cial' usually follows a vowel and '–tial' usually follows a consonant. However, they should also remember there are exceptions to that rule.

Answers

1. *A birthday is a <u>special</u> day.*	[example]
2. This information is <u>confidential</u>.	[1 mark]
3. Water is <u>essential</u> to life.	[1 mark]
4. A smile is a type of <u>facial</u> expression.	[1 mark]
5. The evidence against the defendant is <u>circumstantial</u>.	[1 mark]
6. The ogre's aggressive behaviour was <u>antisocial</u>.	[1 mark]
7. Many communities are <u>multiracial</u>.	[1 mark]
8. Exercise is <u>beneficial</u> to one's health.	[1 mark]
9. Sanjeev was the <u>official</u> winner of the tournament.	[1 mark]
10. The company faced <u>financial</u> ruin.	[1 mark]

Support, embed & challenge

Support

Provide these children with word cards (see Additional resources), picking out those words that will be most useful to them. Read through the words together and clarify their meanings. As you read the words, split them into syllables, helping the children to hear the /shul/ endings.

Ask the children to work through Unit 2 Resource 1: An unofficial outing. (**Answers** /shul/ spelt 'cial': unofficial, special, artificial, beneficial, glacial, crucial; /shul/ spelt 'tial': torrential, initial, potential, substantial, partial) Afterwards, look at the two lists and identify the vowel or consonant before the ending. Return to the story and circle the noun phrases that each /shul/ word is part of. Create new noun phrases for each word from the resource sheet and help the children to write their phrases on their whiteboards, for example: 'unofficial bridesmaid', 'substantial amount of homework', 'potential treat', 'glacial look', 'crucial equipment'.

Embed

Organise the children into small groups and provide the groups with word cards (see Additional resources). Tell them to put the words in a pile, face down in the middle of the group. Tell them to take turns to draw a card and read it out. The first person to correctly spell the ending gets the card. If the first person says the wrong ending, the person who drew the card keeps the card. See who has the most cards at the end.

Ask the children to complete Unit 2 Resource 2: Essen<u>tial</u> words, benefi<u>cial</u> spellings. (**Answers** 1. official, 2. antisocial, 3. essential, 4. beneficial, 5. martial, 6. artificial, 7. initial, 8. influential, 9. confidential, 10. substantial; 1. antisocial, 2. artificial, 3. confidential, 4. crucial, 5. initial, 6. martial, 7. substantial, 8. official, 9. beneficial, 10. influential) Once they have finished, ask them to spot which words follow the vowel + 'cial' and consonant + 'tial' rule. Challenge them to become an expert in spelling the words on the resource sheet, taking turns to test each other in pairs.

Ask the children to create their own noun phrases for the words 'partial', 'essential', 'residential' and 'preferential'.

Challenge

Ask these children to learn the meanings and spellings of the words 'quintessential', 'racial', 'commercial' and 'sequential' and then use them in sentences of their own.

Homework / Additional activities

Spelling test

Ask the children to learn one of the following lists of words for a spelling test. Challenge them to write sentences for five of the words on their list.

Core words	Support words	Challenge words
official	official	official
special	special	special
partial	partial	partial
initial	initial	initial
martial	martial	martial
crucial	crucial	crucial
artificial	artificial	artificial
essential	essential	essential
unofficial	unofficial	unofficial
confidential	confidential	confidential
beneficial		beneficial
antisocial		antisocial
commercial		commercial
		glacial
		influential
		torrential

Collins Connect: Unit 2

Ask the children to complete Unit 2 (see Teach → Year 5 → Spelling → Unit 2).

Unit 3A: The suffixes –ant and –ent

Overview

English curriculum objectives

- Words ending in –ant, –ance/–ancy, –ent, –ence/–ency

Treasure House resources

- Spelling Skills Pupil Book 5, Unit 3A, pages 8–9
- Collins Connect Treasure House Spelling Year 5, Unit 3

- Photocopiable Unit 3A, Resource 1: Impor<u>tant</u> spellings for intelli<u>gent</u> stud<u>ents</u>, page 80
- Photocopiable Unit 3A, Resource 2: Relev<u>ant</u> words, signific<u>ant</u> sentences, page 81

Additional resources

- Counters and dice (for Resource 1)
- Yellow and green colouring pens/pencils/crayons (for Resource 1)

Introduction

Teaching overview

The endings '–ent' and '–ant' sound very similar and there are many words with these endings. Most of these words just have to be learned, but there are some patterns that can help: after the letter 'm', the ending is almost always '–ent', as in 'moment'; after /s/ spelt 'c', /j/ spelt 'g', /kw/ spelt 'qu' or /sh/ spelt 'ci', the ending is usually '–ent', as in 'innocent', 'emergent', 'frequent' and 'ancient'; after /k/ spelt 'c' or /g/ spelt 'g', the ending is '–ant', as in 'applicant' and 'elegant'.

Sometimes related words can provide clues, for example, 'hesit<u>a</u>tion', therefore 'hesit<u>a</u>nt'.

Introduce the concept

Organise the children into groups and give each group a set of words cut out from Unit 3A Resource 1: Impor<u>tant</u> spellings for intelli<u>gent</u> stud<u>ents</u>. Use 'important' and 'silent' to introduce the spelling pattern,

asking volunteers to help you underline the endings. Explain that, most of the time, these two endings sound the same but that there are some patterns that can help them pick the correct ending. Ask the groups to sort their words into '–ent' and '–ant' endings and see if they can see any patterns. Share any patterns the children find. Clarify and confirm the patterns as: '–ent' after 'm', /kw/ spelt 'qu', /s/ spelt 'c', /j/ spelt 'g', and /sh/ spelt 'ci'; '–ant' after /k/ spelt 'c' and /g/ spelt 'g'. Ask the children to find words: ending '–ment' (such as 'movement'); ending 'g' + 'ent' (such as 'intelligent'); ending 'c' + 'ent' (such as 'innocent'); ending 'g' + 'ant' (such as 'elegant'); ending 'c' + 'ant' (such as 'vacant'). Use the examples they find to write a set of rules with examples on the board. Tell each child to choose two '–ent' words and two '–ant' words to learn, using the spelling rules to help them (if the rules apply). Tell them to swap their four words with a partner who must then test them.

Pupil practice

Pupil Book pages 8–9

Get started

In this activity, children sort words into two groups: words ending '–ant' and words ending '–ent'. Afterwards, ask them to learn the words in each list.

Ask the children to write '–ant' on one side of their whiteboards and '–ent' on the other. Tell them to hide their answers to this activity. Read out the words and ask the children to hold up the appropriate ending for each word.

Answers

Words ending '–ant'		Words ending '–ent'	
attendant	*[example]*	independent	[1 mark]
hesitant	[1 mark]	innocent	[1 mark]
observant	[1 mark]	confident	[1 mark]
servant	[1 mark]	agent	[1 mark]
		obedient	[1 mark]
		decent	[1 mark]

Try these

In this activity, children choose the correct spelling of each word. Ensure that the children are familiar enough with these words to be able to recognise the correct spellings. Afterwards, sort the words into the different spelling patterns and write them on the board.

Answers

1. *important*		*[example]*
2. tolerant		[1 mark]
3. expectant		[1 mark]
4. magnificent		[1 mark]
5. absent		[1 mark]
6. different		[1 mark]
7. urgent		[1 mark]
8. intelligent		[1 mark]
9. radiant		[1 mark]
10. president		[1 mark]

Now try these

In this activity, children compose sentences for the target words 'important', 'tolerant', 'expectant', 'magnificent', 'absent', 'different', 'urgent', 'intelligent', 'radiant' and 'president' (from the 'Try these' activity). Ensure that the children understand the meaning of each word. Tell the children to share their ideas with a partner before writing. Afterwards, share the children's sentences.

Suggested answers

The children studied for an important exam. [example]

Accept any sentences where the target word is correctly spelt and used.
[10 marks: 1 mark per sentence]

Support, embed & challenge

Support

Ask these children to complete Unit 3A Resource 1: Important spellings for intelligent students. (**Answers** yellow: parent, experiment, different, accident, agreement, argument, excellent, innocent, movement, competent, present, student, treatment, equipment, comment, intelligent, content, silent, settlement, frequent; green: brilliant, distant, elegant, hesitant, instant, pleasant, relevant, reluctant, significant, tyrant, elephant, constant, vacant, important, arrogant, infant, extravagant, triumphant, assistant, servant) Afterwards, ask the children to cut up their pages into individual words and sort them according to the two endings. Ask them to choose eight words that they want to learn. Give them a few minutes to learn these, then take their words away from them and see how many they can remember.

Read the words on these children's spelling list (see Spelling test). Practise saying each word in a way that emphasises the '–ent' or '–ant' ending.

Embed

Ask the children to complete Unit 3A Resource 2: Relevant words, significant sentences. (**Answers** 1. distant, 2. innocent, 3. important, 4. urgent, 5. relevant, 6. different, 7. accident, 8. significant, 9. excellent, 10. elephant, 11. obedient) Afterwards, tell them to pair up and test each other to see if they can remember the endings of the words on the sheet.

Ask the children to work in pairs and provide each pair with a copy of Unit 3A Resource 1: Important spellings for intelligent students, two counters and a dice. Ask them to place their counters to the left of the word 'settlement' then to take turns to throw the dice and to move the number of spaces dictated by the dice, zigzagging across and up the board. When a player lands on a word, they must close their eyes and spell it. If they are successful, they can remain on the word. If not, they must return to their last word and wait for their next go. The first child to reach the word 'parent' in the top left corner is the winner.

Challenge

Explain to these children that, sometimes, a related word can help us to know when to choose '–ent' and when to choose '–ant', for example, 'hesitation', therefore 'hesitant'. Challenge these children to work as a group to think of related words with /ay/, /a/ or /e/ sounds for as many of the words from Unit 3A Resource 1: Important spellings for intelligent students as they can, for example: 'vacancy', 'innocence', 'accidentally', 'infantile'. Provide dictionaries to help them with their search. Ask them to create a chart to display words ending '–ent' and '–ant' and their related words and ask them to present their chart to the class.

Homework / Additional activities

Spelling test

Ask the children to learn one of the following lists of words for a spelling test. Challenge them to write sentences for five of the words on their list.

Core words	Support words	Challenge words
distant	distant	distant
instant	brilliant	instant
brilliant	important	brilliant
important	elephant	important
elephant	pleasant	significant
pleasant	accident	relevant
triumphant	excellent	elephant
accident	silent	pleasant
excellent	innocent	triumphant
silent	different	accident
innocent		excellent
different		silent
enjoyment		innocent
ingredient		different
intelligent		enjoyment
		ingredient
		intelligent
		ancient

Collins Connect: Unit 3

Ask the children to complete Unit 3 (see Teach → Year 5 → Spelling → Unit 3).

Unit 3B: The suffixes –ence, –ency, –ance and –ancy

Overview

English curriculum objectives

- Words ending in –ant, –ance/–ancy, –ent, –ence/–ency

Treasure House resources

- Spelling Skills Pupil Book 5, Unit 3B, pages 10–11
- Photocopiable Unit 3B, Resource 1: Spell with confid<u>ence</u>, page 82
- Photocopiable Unit 3B, Resource 2: Spell with compet<u>ency</u>, page 83

Additional resources

- Word cards: distant, distance, brilliant, brilliance, important, importance, excellent, excellence, hesitant, hesitance, hesitancy, silent, silence, innocent, innocence, different, difference, entrant, entrance, important, importance, emergent, emergency, urgent, urgency, frequent, frequency, vacant, vacancy, significant, significance, attendant, attendance, ignorant, ignorance, disturbance, sentence, experience, appearance

Introduction

Teaching overview

Following on from adjectives ending '–ent' and '–ant', this unit covers the related nouns ending '–ance', '–ancy', '–ence' and '–ency'. The children should follow the same rules for choosing the 'a' or 'e' spelling as they did for choosing '–ant' or '–ent,' because the nouns take the same 'a' or 'e' spelling as their related '–ant' or '–ent' adjectives. Of course, not all '–ant' or '–ent' words have related '–ance', '–ancy', '–ence' or '–ency' nouns ('elephant', for example). Of those that do, very few take both '–ance'/'–ence' and '–ancy'/'–ency' endings. The children will need to learn which of the endings create a word (though they will already know most of the words they will want to use). For example: 'urgent' → 'urgency' but not 'urgence', 'silent' → 'silence' but not 'silency', 'vacant' → 'vacancy' but not 'vacance', 'important' → 'importance' but not 'importancy'. However, 'hesitant' → 'hesitance' and 'hesitancy'.

Introduce the concept

Organise the children into groups. Give each group a set of word cards (see Additional resources) and ask the children to pair the related words. Wait for them to notice that a few cards do not have a pair (ask them to put these cards to one side) and that there is one trio: 'hesitant', 'hesitance' and 'hesitancy'. Write the trio on the board and use this to introduce the spelling pattern. Underline the ending of each word and explain that 'hesitant' is an adjective, and 'hesitance' and 'hesitancy' are nouns, for example: 'Don't be hesitant.' 'I understand your hesitance but you're quite safe.' 'Your hesitancy is creating a queue! Be brave!' Explain that, unlike 'hesitant', 'hesitance' and 'hesitancy', most of these nouns take either 'ce' or 'cy' endings but not usually both.

Tell the children to work in their groups to choose two pairs of words, one with a 'ce' ending and one with a 'cy' ending, and create sentences for each word.

Ask the children to look at the word cards they put to one side and tell you which words did not have a pair. Write these on the board: 'disturbance', 'sentence', 'experience', 'appearance'. Explain that these words do not have a related '–ant' or '–ent' word.

Pupil practice

Get started

In this activity, children match adjectives ending '–ent' and '–ant' to their related nouns and underline the endings of all the words. Discuss the pairs, pointing out the matching endings. Try out different endings on the nouns and agree that, for example, 'vacance' and 'silency' do not exist.

Answers

1. *innoc<u>ent</u>*	*innoc<u>ence</u>*	*[example]*
2. urg<u>ent</u>	urg<u>ency</u>	[1 mark]
3. eleg<u>ant</u>	eleg<u>ance</u>	[1 mark]
4. confid<u>ent</u>	confid<u>ence</u>	[1 mark]

5. differ<u>ent</u>	differ<u>ence</u>	[1 mark]
6. brilli<u>ant</u>	brilli<u>ance</u>	[1 mark]
7. sil<u>ent</u>	sil<u>ence</u>	[1 mark]
8. vac<u>ant</u>	vac<u>ancy</u>	[1 mark]

Try these

In this activity, children copy and complete the sentences by choosing the correct spelling for each missing word. This activity checks that the children understand the difference between '–ence'/'–ance' and plurals of words ending '–ant' or '–ent'. For each sentence, ask the children to read the two answer options carefully. Point out that one will have a plural 's' and one will be a singular noun. If they are unsure, ask them to try the sentences in the singular.

Answers

1. *Mia and Tia were wearing the same jumper – what a coincidence!*   [example]
2. Put all the ingredients in a bowl and mix them together.   [1 mark]
3. I know you ate the cake because the evidence is all around your mouth!   [1 mark]
4. The elephants destroyed the undergrowth.   [1 mark]
5. The audience clapped loudly at the end of the show.   [1 mark]
6. The servants lined up to meet the new master of the manor.   [1 mark]

Now try these

In this activity, children consider pairs of potential words, each pair ending '–ance' and '–ancy' or '–ence' and '–ency', and decide which word in each pair exists. Ask the children to read the words in the list out loud with a partner before discussing which one they think exists. Ask them to write the real words.

Answers

1. *frequency*   [example]
2. audience   [1 mark]
3. performance   [1 mark]
4. decency   [1 mark]
5. resistance   [1 mark]
6. Presidency   [1 mark]
7. defence   [1 mark]
8. pregnancy   [1 mark]

Support, embed & challenge

Support

Ask these children to complete Unit 3B Resource 1: Spell with confidence. (**Answers** adjectives: infant, expectant, efficient, magnificent, elegant, urgent, intelligent, distant, observant, independent; nouns: infancy, expectancy, efficiency, magnificence, elegance, urgency, intelligence, distance, observance, independence) Afterwards, cut out all the words, muddle them up and ask the children to sort them again. Underline the endings and discuss the 'ce' and 'cy' options. If necessary, clarify the difference between words ending 'ce' and words ending 'ts'.

Read out a list of words, for example, 'presents', 'presence', 'parents', difference', 'giants' and 'licence', and ask the children to write the last two letters of each.

Embed

Ask the children to complete Unit 3B Resource 2: Spell with competency. (**Answers** efficiency, no

word, consequence, violence, no word, elegance, no word, coincident, expectancy, decency, intelligent, confidence, magnificence, ignorant, infancy)

Provide the children with the following list of word beginnings and ask them to complete each word with the correct ending, '–ence', '–ance', '–ency' or '–ancy': 'consequ__', 'viol__', 'intellig__', 'coincid__', 'effici__', 'expect__', 'frequ__', 'obedi__', 'urg__', 'consist__', 'curr__', 'dec__', 'const__', 'occup__', 'fin__', 'insur__', 'adv__', 'subst__'. Allow access to dictionaries for the children to check the spellings.

Challenge

Ask these children to create a poster about the endings '–ence', '–ance', '–ency' or '–ancy' to be displayed in the classroom. Ask them to create a chart with four columns, one for each ending, then write as many words as they can find under each heading.

Homework / Additional activities

Spelling test

Ask the children to learn one of the following lists of words for a spelling test. Challenge them to write sentences for five of the words on their list.

Core words	Support words	Challenge words
distance	distance	distance
importance	importance	importance
entrance	excellence	entrance
disturbance	silence	disturbance
appearance	innocence	appearance
excellence	difference	ignorance
silence	urgency	excellence
innocence	emergency	coincidence
difference	vacancy	silence
intelligence	infancy	innocence
urgency		difference
emergency		intelligence
frequency		urgency
vacancy		emergency
infancy		frequency
		vacancy
		infancy
		fluency

Unit 3C: Common words (1)

Overview

English curriculum objectives
- Word list – Years 5 and 6

Treasure House resources
- Spelling Skills Pupil Book 5, Unit 3C, pages 12–13
- Photocopiable Unit 3C, Resource 1: Appreciate these excellent words!, page 84
- Photocopiable Unit 3C, Resource 2: Excellent words to communicate with, page 85

Additional resources
- Word cards: accommodate, accompany, according, aggressive, apparent, appreciate, attached, committee, communicate, community, correspond, embarrass, exaggerate, excellent, immediate
- A bag to draw word cards from

Introduction

Teaching overview
This unit covers 15 words, all with double letters, from the list of words for Years 5 and 6: 'accommodate', 'accompany', 'according', 'aggressive', 'apparent', 'appreciate', 'attached', 'committee', 'communicate', 'community', 'correspond', 'embarrass', 'exaggerate', 'excellent' and 'immediate'. In some respects, it is the single letters in these words that cause problems as children begin to double letters with abandon. They know there is a double letter but cannot remember which one it is.

Introduce the concept
Give a set of word cards to each group and ask the children to underline the double letter in each word.

Point out that some words have two sets of double letters. Ask them to decide which other letters will cause them problems, for example, the single 'r' in 'apparent'. Tell them to use a highlighter to highlight those letters.

Put all the word cards in a bag. Ask a child to draw a card from the bag and challenge you to write the word correctly on the board. Misspell the word. Invite the children to check your spelling and tell you how to write the word correctly. Repeat the process with the rest of the words, sometimes misspelling them and sometimes writing them correctly.

Pupil practice

Pupil Book pages 12–13

Get started
In this activity, children sort words into three groups: words with a double 'm', words with a double 'c' and words with a double 'p'. Ask the children to find the double letters in the words. Tell them to look out for one word that will appear on two lists.

Answers

Double 'm'	Double 'c'	Double 'p'
committee [example]	accompany [1 mark]	appreciate [1 mark]
accommodate [1 mark]	accommodate [1 mark]	apparent [1 mark]
communicate [1 mark]	according [1 mark]	
community [1 mark]		
immediate [1 mark]		

Try these
In this activity, children look at two spelling options and choose the correct one. Tell them to pay close attention to which letters are double and which are single. Remind them that double letters do not usually occur with another consonant.

Answers
1. attached — [example]
2. excellent — [1 mark]
3. exaggerate — [1 mark]
4. embarrass — [1 mark]
5. correspond — [1 mark]
6. accompany — [1 mark]
7. aggressive — [1 mark]
8. immediate — [1 mark]

Now try these

In this activity, children copy and complete sentences by filling in the missing letter or letters in words with double letters. Ask the children to work out what the word with missing letters is. Tell them to write a single or a double letter where each gap is to complete the word correctly.

Answers

1. *I'm so embarrassed!*   *[example]*
2. Come here immediately.   [2 marks]
3. Can you accompany us please?   [2 marks]
4. That's excellent!   [2 marks]
5. Ravi and Ben are on the committee.   [2 marks]
6. According to Casey, you have my ball.   [2 marks]

Support, embed & challenge

Support

Ask the children to complete Unit 3C Resource 1: Appreciate these excellent words! (**Answers (page 1)**)
1. [a][cc][o][m][p][a][n][y], 2. [a][cc][or][d][i][ng],
3. [a][tt][a][ch][ed], 4. [c][o][mm][i][tt][ee],
5. [c][o][mm][u][n][i][t][y], 6. [c][o][rr][e][s][p][o][n][d],
7. [e][m][b][a][rr][a][ss], 8. [a][pp][a][r][e][n][t])
Afterwards, ask them to write the remaining words ('accommodate', 'aggressive', 'appreciate', 'communicate', 'exaggerate', 'excellent', 'immediate') in the same style. Discuss the spellings, focusing in particular on the single letters. Talk about how the children can remember which letters should be double and which should be single.

As a group, practise spelling the words using Unit 3C Resource 2: Excellent words to communicate with.

Embed

Tell the children to create a poster of the key words to display at home. Tell them to write the words down the centre of the page using different colours for double letters, tricky single letters and the other letters, for example, green for double letters, red for tricky single letters and black for the rest. Suggest that they decorate their posters.

Provide the children with a set of word cards (see Additional resources). Tell them to place them face down and take turns to pick up a card and test their partner. If the partner spells the word correctly, their partner can keep the card. The person with the most cards at the end is the winner.

Ask the children to complete Unit 3C Resource 2: Excellent words to communicate with to practise spelling these words.

Challenge

Ask these children to write a sentence for each word, for example: 'According to the master, I must accompany you to the accommodation.' 'It is apparent that you appreciate apples.'

Tell the children to use these words to play a game of Hangman with a partner.

Homework / Additional activities

Spelling test

Ask the children to learn the following list. Challenge them to write sentences for five of the words on their list.

accommodate	communicate
accompany	community
according	correspond
aggressive	embarrass
apparent	exaggerate
appreciate	excellent
attached	immediate
committee	

# Unit 4: The suffixes –able, –ible, –ably and –ibly

Overview

English curriculum objectives

- Words ending in –able and –ible; words ending in –ably and –ibly

Treasure House resources

- Spelling Skills Pupil Book 5, Unit 4, pages 14–15
- Collins Connect Treasure House Spelling Year 5, Unit 4
- Photocopiable Unit 4, Resource 1: Are you able to add ible and able?, page 86
- Photocopiable Unit 4, Resource 2: Sensible words spelt predictably, page 87

Additional resources

- Adjective cards: comfortable, reasonable, dependable, enjoyable, understandable, miserable, remarkable, horrible, possible, terrible, invisible, incredible, sensible, responsible, feasible
- Adverb cards: comfortably, reasonably, dependably, enjoyably, understandably, miserably, remarkably, horribly, possibly, terribly, invisibly, incredibly, sensibly, responsibly, feasibly
- A bag to draw word cards from

Introduction

Teaching overview

When deciding whether to spell an ending '–ible' or '–able', it is useful to note that, when the complete root word remains, the ending is often '–able', for example, 'adorable', 'acceptable' and 'imaginable'. When the root of the word is not a complete word, the ending is usually '–ible', such as 'illegible' and 'irascible'. The endings '–ible' and '–able' create adjectives; the endings '–ibly' and '–ably' create adverbs. This unit focuses on words with a complete or partial root. More complex arrangements will be confronted in Year 6.

Introduce the concept

Organise the children into groups and provide each group with a set of adjective cards (see Additional resources). Ask them to sort the cards into two piles: words ending '–ible' and words ending '–able'. Tell them to read the words and discuss the meanings together in their groups. Once they have done so, ask each group to share any words they do not know with the rest of the class. Invite children from other groups to volunteer definitions for the unknown words and then provide definitions for those words nobody knows. Ask: 'What sort of words are these?' (adjectives) Explain that: if you are **able** to hear the complete root word, the ending is (usually) '–able'; if the root word is only a fragment, the ending is (usually) '–ible'.

Ask the children to look at each word and decide if it does or does not fit the rule. Tell them to work together in their groups with each group member taking responsibility for a few words.

Give each group a set of adverb cards. Challenge the children to identify what sort of words these '–ibly' and '–ably' words are. Establish that they are adverbs. Demonstrate how to use them with sentences, such as: 'He slept comfortably in the new bed.' 'He threw the ball terribly'. Ask them to match up the pairs of related adjectives and adverbs.

Pupil practice

Pupil Book pages 14–15

Get started

In this activity, children copy and complete a table, filling in the missing root, related adjective and/or related adverb for each word. Provide support for this exercise if necessary. Afterwards, discuss the meanings of the words, providing example sentences.

Answers

Root		Adjective		Adverb	
comfort	*[example]*	*comfortable*	*[example]*	comfortably	
consider		considerable	[1 mark]	considerably	[1 mark]
understand	[1 mark]	understandable		understandably	[1 mark]
reason	[1 mark]	reasonable	[1 mark]	reasonably	
enjoy	[1 mark]	enjoyable		enjoyably	[1 mark]
laugh		laughable	[1 mark]	laughably	[1 mark]

Try these

In this activity, children write the correct spelling of each word, choosing between the '–ible' or '–able' endings. Tell the children to say each word, testing which ending sounds right. Remind them of the rule: clear root + 'able'; word fragment + 'ible'. All the words here follow this rule. Afterwards, use these words to reinforce the rule.

Answers

1. *possible*		*[example]*
2. incredible		[1 mark]
3. reasonable		[1 mark]
4. honourable		[1 mark]
5. terrible		[1 mark]
6. edible		[1 mark]
7. horrible		[1 mark]
8. visible		[1 mark]
9. dependable		[1 mark]
10. bearable		[1 mark]

Now try these

In this activity, children change the verbs 'sense', 'consider', 'comfort', 'laugh', 'honour', 'bear', 'depend', 'avoid' and 'afford' into adjectives or adverbs (they can choose which) and then use them in sentences of their own devising. Recap the rules for turning these words into adjectives and adverbs. Check that the children have correctly formed their words before they proceed to write sentences.

Suggested answers

"Line up sensibly," the teacher said. [example]

Accept any sentences where the target word is correctly spelt and used.

adjectives: sensible, considerable, comfortable, laughable, honourable, bearable, dependable, avoidable, affordable

adverbs: sensibly, considerably, comfortably, laughably, honourably, bearably, dependably, avoidably, affordably

[1 mark per adjective or adverb correctly formed from the target word; 1 mark per sentence]

Support, embed & challenge

Support

Put the adjective cards in a bag and ask the children to take turns to pull out a word and read it out. Make up a short sentence using the word before the next word is drawn, for example: 'This chair is not comfortable.' 'It's not reasonable to shout at me.' After a while, swap roles, with you drawing the word cards and the children working together to make up sentences.

Recap on the rule for adding '–able' and '–ible' to complete words and partial words: for complete words, use '–able'; for word fragments, use '–ible'. Cut the endings off the words on the cards and challenge the children to recreate the words.

Ask the children to complete Unit 4 Resource 1: Are you <u>able</u> to add <u>ible</u> and <u>able</u>? (**Answers** words ending '–ible': incredible, responsible, defensible, horrible, terrible, invisible, impossible; words ending '–able': reasonable, remarkable, miserable, suitable, noticeable, comfortable, acceptable, payable, profitable)

Embed

Draw the following grid on the board. Remind the children of the 'Get started' activity they completed in the Pupil Book. Explain that partial root words are in brackets.

Root	Adjective	Adverb
	flexible	
(respons)		responsibly
depend		
		miserably
remark		
(poss)		

Once the children have copied and completed the grid, ask them to practise using the words in sentences.

Ask the children to complete Unit 4 Resource 2: Sens<u>ible</u> words spelt predict<u>ably</u>. (**Answers** flexibly, forcibly, inevitably, remarkably, terribly, comfortably, suitably, incredibly, sensibly, arguably, understandably, visibly, uncomfortably, impossibly, noticeably, horribly, miserably, responsibly, predictably, forcibly, improbably, memorably)

Challenge

Provide these children with the following pairs of words: 'response' and 'responsible', 'desire' and 'desirable', 'note' and 'notable', 'value' and 'valuable'. Challenge them to work out what the rule is for adding '–able' and '–ible' to words ending in 'e'.

Homework / Additional activities

Spelling test

Ask the children to learn one of the following lists of words for a spelling test. Challenge them to write sentences for five of the words on their list.

Core words	Support words	Challenge words
valuable	valuable	valuable
unable	unable	unable
reasonable	reasonable	reasonable
remarkable	remarkable	remarkable
available	available	available
possible	possible	incredible
incredible	incredible	responsible
terrible	terrible	flexible
responsible	horrible	miserable
invisible	invisible	suitable
inevitably		inevitably
reasonably		reasonably
remarkably		arguably
noticeably		remarkably
incredibly		noticeably
		incredibly
		audibly
		defensibly

Collins Connect: Unit 4

Ask the children to complete Unit 4 (see Teach → Year 5 → Spelling → Unit 4).

Unit 5: Adding suffixes beginning with vowels to words ending in –fer

Overview

English curriculum objectives

- Adding suffixes beginning with vowel letters to words ending in –fer

Treasure House resources

- Spelling Skills Pupil Book 5, Unit 5, pages 16–17
- Collins Connect Treasure House Spelling Year 5, Unit 5
- Photocopiable Unit 5, Resource 1: <u>Suffering</u> from stress, page 88
- Photocopiable Unit 5, Resource 2: Can you hear the <u>difference</u>? page 89

Additional resources

- Word cards: suffered, suffering, proffered, proffering, buffered, buffering, preferred, preferring, preference, offered, offering, referred, referring, reference, conferred, conferring, conference, transferred, transferring, transference, deferred, deferring, deference, differed, differing, difference, inferred, inferring, inference
- Red and yellow colouring pens/pencils/crayons (for Resource 1)

Introduction

Teaching overview

When adding '–ed', '–ing' or '–ence' to words ending in '–fer', the children need to learn which words need a double 'r' and which do not. Words with an unstressed '–fer' have a single 'r' before the suffix, for example, 'suff<u>e</u>red', 'inf<u>e</u>rence' and 'off<u>e</u>ring'. Words that have the stress on the '–fer' syllable need a double 'r' before the suffix, for example, 'def<u>err</u>ed' and 'ref<u>err</u>ing'. In general, a double 'r' is more common before 'ed' and 'ing' and a single 'r' is more common before '–ence'. Because the rule applies to words after the suffix has been added, related words do not always have the same spelling pattern, for example, 'conf<u>err</u>ing' but 'conf<u>e</u>rence'.

Introduce the concept

Organise the children into groups. Give each group of children a set of word cards (see Additional resources). Ask them to work as a team to underline the part of the word with the strongest stress. Warn them that related words will not necessarily have the same stress. Next, ask them to sort the words into those with 'fer' (single 'r') before the suffix and those with 'ferr' (double 'r') before the suffix. Ask: 'Can you see a pattern?' Write some of the words from the cards on the board and use these to explain the spelling rule: unstressed 'fer' = single 'r', for example, 'suff<u>e</u>red' and 'conf<u>e</u>rence'; stressed 'ferr' = double 'rr', for example, 'conf<u>err</u>ed' and 'ref<u>err</u>ing'.

Ask the children to re-sort their word cards into pairs or trios of related words, for example, 'conferred', 'conferring', 'conference'. Ask them whether the related words have the same stress patterns. Agree that they do not: the stress is different with the '–ence' ending and these words almost never have a double 'r' after 'fer'.

Pupil practice

Pupil Book pages 16–17

Get started

In this activity, children add '–ed' to words, deciding whether each word should be spelt with a single or a double 'r'. Ask the children to say each word with the suffix and listen to the stresses before writing the word down.

Answers

1. *suffered*	*[example]*
2. offered	[1 mark]
3. preferred	[1 mark]
4. referred	[1 mark]
5. inferred	[1 mark]

'–fer' is stressed with suffix		'–fer' is not stressed with suffix	
preferred	[1 mark]	suffered	[1 mark]
referred	[1 mark]	offered	[1 mark]
inferred	[1 mark]		

Try these

In this activity, children choose the correct spelling of each word. Tell the children to read each word carefully out loud to determine where the stress lies and so work out the spelling.

Answers

1. *suffering*		*[example]*
2. offering		[1 mark]
3. conferring		[1 mark]
4. preferring		[1 mark]
5. reference		[1 mark]
6. preference		[1 mark]
7. referring		[1 mark]
8. transferring		[1 mark]
9. referral		[1 mark]
10. referee		[1 mark]

Now try these

In this activity, children copy a paragraph and fill in the missing letters in words that end 'fer' or 'ferr' + suffix. Read the paragraph together a couple of times, agreeing on what the missing words are. Check that the children understand the words and the context of the words. Correct any mispronunciation. Point out that the last word adds the suffix '–al' but that the same rules apply.

Answers

The waiter *offered* the customers a drink. After con**ferr**ing briefly, they said they normally pre**ferr**ed to see the menu first. The waiter re**ferr**ed them to the specials board, took their orders and, in re**fer**ence to the soup, made a note of the woman's pre**fer**ence. However, while trans**ferr**ing their meal from tray to table, the waiter su**ffer**ed a fall. From the looks on their faces, the waiter in**ferr**ed they would not give the restaurant a good re**ferr**al.

[9 marks: 1 mark for each correctly completed word]

Support, embed & challenge

Support

Read the words on the word cards (see Additional resources) and repeat the activities from the 'Introduce the concept' session with this group. Check that they can hear the stressed syllable and understand the link to the spelling pattern.

Ask the children to complete Unit 5 Resource 1: Suffering from stress. (**Answers** red: inferring, preferring, transferring, preferred, transferred, referral, preferred; yellow: suffering, buffering, offered, differing, preference, pilfering, offering, suffered, referee, difference, proffered, inference; not coloured: buffer, proffer, pilfer)

Embed

Ask the children to complete Unit 5 Resource 2: Can you hear the difference? Tell the children to say the words aloud before writing them down. Advise them to listen carefully to the different stress patterns to ascertain whether or not to double the 'r'. (**Answers** defer: deferred, deferring, deference; refer: referring, referred, reference; differ: differing, differed, difference; confer: conferring, conferred, conference; transfer: transferring, transferred, transference; infer: inferring, inferred, inference; prefer: preferring, preferred, preference) After the children have completed their table, ask them if they can see a prevalence of any spelling pattern in each column. Check the children understand each word, in particular 'deference' and 'transference'. Challenge them to they work out the meanings from their knowledge of the root words.

Challenge

Provide the children with a set of word cards (see Additional resources). Remind them that 'ferr' is more frequent before '–ed' and '–ing' and 'fer' is more frequent before '–ence'. Ask them to find all the exceptions to this different way of looking at the spelling pattern. Ask: 'How many words do not fit this new rule?' Suggest that, if they find this easier, they should just learn these exception words. Ask them to create a poster describing the alternative rule (with examples) and listing the exception words. Display their posters in the classroom.

Homework / Additional activities

Spelling test

Ask the children to learn one of the following lists of words for a spelling test. Challenge them to write sentences for five of the words on their list.

Core words	Support words	Challenge words
suffered	suffered	suffering
suffering	suffering	buffered
buffered	buffered	buffering
buffering	buffering	preferred
preferred	offered	preference
preference	offering	offered
offered	difference	offering
offering	inferring	transferred
transferred	inference	differing
differing	referred	difference
difference		inferring
infer		inference
inferring		pilfered
inference		pilfering
		proffered
		proffering

Collins Connect: Unit 5

Ask the children to complete Unit 5 (see Teach → Year 5 → Spelling → Unit 5).

Review unit 1

A. Children choose the correct spelling for each word.

Answers

1. spacious [1 mark]

2. artificial [1 mark]

3. important [1 mark]

4. accident [1 mark]

5. suitable [1 mark]

6. reference [1 mark]

7. reasonably [1 mark]

8. committee [1 mark]

B. Children look at the incorrectly spelt words and find the spelling mistake.
They then write the correct spelling.

Answers

1. accommodate [1 mark]

2. correspond [1 mark]

3. entrance [1 mark]

4. horrible [1 mark]

5. referred [1 mark]

6. delicious [1 mark]

7. urgency [1 mark]

8. correspond [1 mark]

C. Children copy each sentence and add one of the endings –tial, –ed, –able, –ence, –ant or –ible to complete the word in brackets. They should use each ending only once.

Answers

1. Sleeping on the floor is not very comfort<u>able</u>. [1 mark]

2. Listen, everyone, I have some import<u>ant</u> news. [1 mark]

3. Sacha offer<u>ed</u> her seat on the bus to the old man. [1 mark]

4. The comprehension exercise tested our use of infer<u>ence</u>. [1 mark]

5. Megan is very flex<u>ible</u> and can easily touch her toes. [1 mark]

6. The torrent<u>ial</u> rain ruined our day out. [1 mark]

Unit 6A: Common words (2)

Overview

English curriculum objectives
- Word list – Years 5 and 6

Treasure House resources
- Spelling Skills Pupil Book 5, Unit 6A, pages 20–21
- Photocopiable Unit 6A, Resource 1: <u>Marvellous</u> words to <u>occupy</u> you, page 90
- Photocopiable Unit 6A, Resource 2: An <u>opportunity</u> to learn <u>necessary</u> spellings, page 91

Additional resources
- Word cards: immediately, interrupt, necessary, occupy, occur, opportunity, profession, programme, recommend, suggest, marvellous
- Word cards from Unit 3C: accommodate, accompany, according, aggressive, apparent, appreciate, attached, committee, communicate, community, correspond, embarrass, exaggerate, excellent, immediate

Introduction

Teaching overview

This unit covers another 11 words with double letters from the list of words for Years 5 and 6: 'immediately', 'interrupt', 'necessary', 'occupy', 'occur', 'opportunity', 'profession', 'programme', 'recommend', 'suggest', 'marvellous'. As with the previous words, it is some of the single letters that catch children out, for example: Does 'necessary' have one 'c' or two? As ever, practice makes perfect.

Introduce the concept

Challenge the children to remember some of the tricky words with double letters they learned in Unit 3C: 'accommodate', 'accompany', 'according', 'aggressive', 'apparent', 'appreciate', 'attached', 'committee', 'communicate', 'community',

'correspond', 'embarrass', 'exaggerate', 'excellent', 'immediate'. If they are reticent about offering any spellings, model spelling the words for them, describing your spelling decisions out loud. Introduce the new tricky words with double letters: 'immediately', 'interrupt', 'necessary', 'occupy', 'occur', 'opportunity', 'profession', 'programme', 'recommend', 'suggest' and 'marvellous'. Organise the children into groups and provide them with word cards for the new words (see Additional resources). Ask them to find and underline the double letters in each word and also to pinpoint any potentially troublesome single letters. Focus for a moment on the spelling of 'necessary'. Point out that the single 'c' stands for a /s/ sound. If it were 'cc' it would indicate a /k/, as it does in 'occur', 'accommodate', 'accompany', 'according', and so on.

Pupil practice

Pupil Book pages 20–21

Get started

In this activity, children write out words and underline the double letters in each word. Afterwards, discuss with the children ways of remembering these.

Answers

1. *immediately*	*[example]*
2. interrupt	[1 mark]
3. necessary	[1 mark]
4. occupy	[1 mark]
5. occur	[1 mark]
6. opportunity	[1 mark]
7. profession	[1 mark]
8. programme	[1 mark]
9. recommend	[1 mark]
10. suggest	[1 mark]
11. marvellous	[1 mark]

Try these

In this activity, children copy and complete words, filling in the gaps with single or double consonants. Ensure the children have covered up the words in the 'Get started' activity. Challenge them to remember if the gaps represent a double or single letter – and which letter.

Answers

1. *opportunity*	*[example]*
2. programme	[1 mark]
3. interrupt	[1 mark]
4. marvellous	[1 mark]
5. occupy	[1 mark]

6. recommend [1 mark]

7. immediately [1 mark]

8. occur [1 mark]

9. necessary [1 mark]

10. profession [1 mark]

11. suggest [1 mark]

Now try these

In this activity, children copy and complete sentences, choosing the correct spelling of the missing words.

Answers

1. *We had a marvellous day out at the zoo.* [example]

2. Please don't <u>interrupt</u> me – I'm talking to Mrs Bishop. [1 mark]

3. It's cold and wet so I <u>recommend</u> you take a coat. [1 mark]

4. Ben slipped and, suddenly, Oliver had an <u>opportunity</u> to score. [1 mark]

5. It's going to be <u>necessary</u> to drive into town because we're late. [1 mark]

Support, embed & challenge

Support

Read the target words carefully with these children, picking out the double and single letters.

Ask the children to complete Unit 6A Resource 1: <u>Marvellous</u> words to <u>occupy</u> you. (**Answers** 1. *[i][mm][e][d][i][a][t][e][l][y] [example]*, 2. [i][n][t][err][u][p][t], 3. [n][e][c][e][ss][a][r][y], 4. [o][cc] [u][p][y], 5. [o][pp][or][t][u][n][i][t][y], 6. [p][r][o][g][r][a] [mm][e], 7. [s][u][gg][e][s][t], 8. [m][ar][v][e][ll][ou][s])

Cut out and display the words from Unit 6A Resource 2: An <u>opportunity</u> to learn <u>necessary</u> spellings and, as a group, pair up words with the same double letters. (**Answers** according, accompany, occupy and occur; exaggerate and suggest; excellent and marvellous; immediate, community, committee, communicate, immediately, programme, recommend and accommodate; apparent and appreciate; correspond and interrupt; embarrass, necessary, profession and aggressive) Muddle the words up, turn them over and use them to play a game of Pairs with the children.

Embed

Ask the children to write out their spelling list (see Spelling test) as a poster to display at home. Tell them to use one colour for any double letters, another for any potentially tricky single letters, and a third colour for the rest. Encourage them to decorate their posters.

Ask the children to complete Unit 6A Resource 1: <u>Marvellous</u> words to <u>occupy</u> you. (**Answers** see above)

Once the children feel confident in their spellings, ask them to work together in pairs and provide the pairs with the word cards for this unit and word cards from Unit 3A, shuffled (see Additional resources). Tell the children to place the cards face down in a pile and take turns to pick up a card and then test their partner on the spelling of the word on the card.

Ask the children to remain in pairs (or organise them into new pairs). Provide the pairs of children with a copy of Unit 6A Resource 2: An <u>opportunity</u> to learn <u>necessary</u> spellings and allow time for them to play the game a couple of times. (**Answers** see above)

Challenge

Provide these children with a list of the words covered in this unit and in Unit 3A (see Additional resources for a comprehensive list). Challenge them to write other words in the same family for as many of the words as possible, for example: 'interrupt' → 'interrupted', 'interrupting', 'interruption'; 'necessary' → 'necessity', 'necessarily', 'unnecessary', 'unnecessarily'; 'occupy' → 'occupied', 'occupation', 'occupational'; 'occur' → 'occurred', 'occurring', 'occurrence'; 'profession' → 'professional', 'professionally'; 'marvellous' → 'marvel', 'marvelled', 'marvelling'.

Homework / Additional activities

Spelling test

Ask the children to learn the following list of words. Challenge them to write sentences for five of the words.

immediately	profession
interrupt	programme
necessary	recommend
occupy	suggest
occur	marvellous
opportunity	

Unit 6B: Use of the hyphen after prefixes

Overview

English curriculum objectives
- Use of the hyphen

Treasure House resources
- Spelling Skills Pupil Book 5, Unit 6B, pages 22–23
- Collins Connect Treasure House Spelling Year 5, Unit 6
- Photocopiable Unit 6B, Resource 1: Re-examining hyphens, page 92

- Photocopiable Unit 6B, Resource 2: Re-enforcing good hyphenation, page 93

Additional resources
- Word cards: anti, co, co, ex, ex, pre, pre, re, re, re, re, re, re, re, self, self, self, un, un, un, aging, assess, assured, bully, collected, controlled, cover, doubt, educated, elected, election, explained, gravity, heat, member, operate, owned, pilot, tie, wind

Introduction

Teaching overview

Unlike other spelling rules taught at this level, the use of the hyphen has an element of personal choice and judgement, and that can be a bit tricky to teach. On the whole, most words with prefixes do not need a hyphen but it is clearer to use a hyphen:

- to separate a prefix and a root word where the combination has resulted in a double vowel, for example, 'co-own', 're-enter', 'anti-immigration'.

- to separate a prefix and a root word where the combination is unusual or hard to read, or to emphasise the prefix, for example, 'anti-aging', 'pre-adolescent', 'de-ice'. (But there are many common words that have lost their hyphen, such as 'coordinate', 'reanimate', 'reassure' and 'reassert'.)

- to distinguish from a known word with a different meaning, for example, 'redress' (create balance) and 're-dress' (to dress again), 'recover' (to get better) and 're-cover' (to cover again), 'recollect' (remember) and 're-collect' (collect again).

- with the prefixes 'ex–' (when it means former) and 'self–' (for example, 'ex-parrot' or 'self-aware') and often, but not always, with the prefix 'anti–' (for example, 'anti-establishment').

In general, children should use a hyphen if it will help the reader.

Introduce the concept

Give each child a word or prefix card (see Additional resources) and ask them to identify whether they have a word or a prefix. Ask the children with prefix cards to find a partner with a word card. They should put their cards together to make a word and then write it down. Ask the children to repeat the activity three more times. Then ask them to share the words they have made and write them on the board. Reject any that are nonsense and hyphenate any that need hyphenating. Add any useful combinations the children may have missed. When you have enough words, sort the words into those with hyphens and those without, and explain the rules.

Pupil practice

Pupil Book pages 22–23

Get started

In this activity, children sort words into two groups: words that are hyphenated and words that are not hyphenated. Discuss how all the words seem to break the rules. Agree that the hyphenated words look odd without a hyphen. Look at the words without a hyphen and agree that all these words are well known and recognisable without a hyphen. These words are not spelt with a hyphen and the children need to remember these spellings.

Answers

Hyphenated		Not hyphenated	
co-worker	[example]	reactivate	[1 mark]
co-star	[1 mark]	react	[1 mark]
ice-cream	[1 mark]	deactivate	[1 mark]
non-stop	[1 mark]	coincidence	[1 mark]
co-pilot	[1 mark]	uncoordinated	[1 mark]

Try these

In this activity, children copy and complete a table, sorting words into two groups: those that need no hyphen and those that do need a hyphen. They add hyphens to the words that need them and write them in the second column of the table. After the children have completed the task, discuss the word 'remove'. Explain that, in this context, it means 'take away'. However, if we wanted to say 'move again' we would need to use a hyphen to emphasise the meaning.

Answers

No hyphen needed		Hyphen needed	
hyperactive	*[example]*	*de-energised*	*[example]*
retry	[1 mark]	pre-exist	[1 mark]
reheat	[1 mark]	ultra-awake	[1 mark]
uninviting	[1 mark]	re-enter	[1 mark]
remove	[1 mark]	re-enact	[1 mark]

Now try these

In this activity, children decide whether to hyphenate words and, if using a hyphen, where the hyphen should be placed in the words. Remind the children to look for double vowels and well-known exceptions.

Answers

1. *ultra-organised*	*[example]*
2. co-exist	[1 mark]
3. unfriendly	[1 mark]
4. co-own	[1 mark]
5. remember	[1 mark]
6. coordination	[1 mark]
7. reheat	[1 mark]
8. revise	[1 mark]
9. return	[1 mark]
10. re-enter	[1 mark]

Support, embed & challenge

Support

Place all the word and prefix cards (see Additional resources) in the middle of the table and work together to add prefixes to roots to create words. Write the words you create and discuss whether or not each word should be hyphenated. Apart from very common words, such as 'reassured' and 'cooperate', hyphenate the words where the combination of prefix and root word has resulted in a double vowel, for example, 'anti-aging' and 'pre-owned'. Also, hyphenate any strange or new words, even if they do not have a double vowel.

Ask the children to complete Unit 6B Resource 1: Re-examining hyphens. All the words in this list with double vowels are hyphenated. (**Answers** re-examine, remember, co-opt, unkind, re-enact, re-enforce, co-own, co-author, pre-election, defrost, ex-president, re-enter, recover, re-educate, reheat, re-evaluate, unpack, re-explain, return)

Embed

Organise the children into groups and provide each group with a set of word and prefix cards (see Additional resources). Ask the groups to spend time creating words, and deciding whether to use a hyphen. Ask each group to create ten words and, writing their words on a whiteboard, to decide whether to hyphenate the prefix and root. Explain that they can use prefixes and roots more than once (for example, 're-elected' and 'unelected') and that sometimes they can make two different words just by adding the hyphen ('recollected' and 're-collected', 'recover' and 're-cover'). When all the groups have made ten words, tell the children to move around the room, looking at the words the other groups have put together.

Provide the children with their spelling list (see Spelling test) and ask them to decide why each word is or is not hyphenated. When they are confident with their words, ask them to complete Unit 6B Resource 2: Re-enforcing good hyphenation. This resource practises recognising which words need hyphens and which, by convention, do not. (**Answers** antivenom or anti-venom, co-author, coeducation or co-education, co-star, de-ice, nonstop, co-pilot, cooperate or co-operate, coordinate or co-ordinate, non-stick, coincidence, co-opt, co-own, reappear, ex-president, reassure, re-educate, recollect (remember) or re-collect (collect again), recover (convalesce) or re-cover (cover again), re-enact, re-energise, re-enforce, re-enter, nonsense, re-evaluate, re-explain, reheat, ice-cream, remember, return (go back) or re-turn (turn again), re-examine, unkind, pre-election, unpack)

Challenge

Ask these children to create a list of words that need hyphens and a list of words that do not. Tell them to design the lists as posters to display in the class.

Ask these children to investigate using hyphens in numbers and using hyphens to avoid ambiguity in sentences, for example: 'I have a great grandmother'.

Homework / Additional activities

Spelling test

Ask the children to learn one of the following lists of words for a spelling test. Challenge them to write sentences for five of the words on their list.

Core words	Support words	Challenge words
co-star	co-star	co-star
coincidence	coincidence	co-pilot
cooperate	cooperate	coincidence
coordinate	ice-cream	cooperate
ice-cream	non-stop	coordinate
non-stop	nonsense	ice-cream
nonsense	reappear	non-stop
reappear	reassure	nonsense
reassure	re-enact	reappear
re-enact	re-enforce	reassure
re-enforce		readjust
re-examine		re-enact
ex-president		re-enforce
anti-bullying		re-examine
		ex-president
		anti-bullying
		anti-venom

Collins Connect: Unit 6

Ask the children to complete Unit 6 (see Teach → Year 5 → Spelling → Unit 6).

Unit 7A: The /ee/ sound spelt ei after c

Overview

English curriculum objectives
- Words with the /ee/ sound spelt ei after c

Treasure House resources
- Spelling Skills Pupil Book 5, Unit 7A, pages 24–25
- Collins Connect Treasure House Spelling Year 5, Unit 7
- Photocopiable Unit 7A, Resource 1: Seize the ei spelling!, page 94
- Photocopiable Unit 7A, Resource 2: Let neither /ee/ spelling give you grief, page 95

Additional resources
- Word cards: niece, chief, believe, hygienic, fields, shield, piece, bunnies, cherries, grief, yield, field, shield, brief, relieved, achieve, retrieve, shriek, deceive, conceive, receive, perceive, ceiling, receipt, deceitful, conceited, seize, neither, either, caffeine
- A bag to draw word cards from
- Yellow colouring pens/pencils/crayons (for Resource 1)

Introduction

Teaching overview

The rule "'i' before 'e' except after 'c'" is useful for remembering how to spell words where the /ee/ sound does not follow a 'c', such as 'Charlie', 'baddie', 'chief', 'shield', 'niece', 'belief', 'piece' and 'grief'. There are only five root words where the /ee/ sound does follow a 'c': 'deceive', 'conceive', 'receive', 'perceive' and 'ceiling'. The first four of these also give us 'deceit', 'deceitful', 'deceitfully', 'undeceive', 'receipt', 'receivers', 'conceit', 'conceited', 'conceitedly', 'conceivable', 'misconceive', and so on.

Words that do not fit the rule are: 'protein', 'caffeine', 'seize', 'either' and 'neither' (unless the 'ei' in 'either' and 'neither' is pronounced /eye/, in which case the rule is irrelevant as it applies exclusively to spelling the /ee/ sound).

Introduce the concept

Give each child one of the word cards (see Additional resources). Ask them to read their word and underline the two letters that represent the /ee/ sound. Ask the children to compare their word with the words other children have. Ask them to work together to sort their words into those spelt 'ie' and those spelt 'ei'. Ask the children with words where /ee/ is spelt 'ei' to come to the front and write their word on the board. Sort the words into those that follow 'c' and those that do not. Introduce the rule "'i' before 'e' except after 'c'" and show how the words where 'ei' follows 'c' fit this rule. Ask the children with /ee/ spelt 'ie' whether their words fit the rule. Point out that, to use this rule, they must also remember the exceptions to the rule: 'protein', 'caffeine', 'seize', 'either' and 'neither'.

Pupil practice

Pupil Book pages 24–25

Get started

In this activity, children sort words into two groups: those with /ee/ spelt 'ei' and those with /ee/ spelt 'ie'. Afterwards, ask which words fit the rule "'i' before 'e' except after 'c'"? (All of them.)

Answers

'i' before 'e'		'e' before 'i'	
grief	[example]	ceiling	[1 mark]
grieving	[1 mark]	deceit	[1 mark]
piece	[1 mark]	receive	[1 mark]
achieve	[1 mark]		
yield	[1 mark]		
belief	[1 mark]		
believe	[1 mark]		

Try these

In this activity, children choose the correct spelling of each word. Ensure that the children are familiar enough with these words to be able to recognise the correct spelling. Afterwards, sort the words into the different spelling patterns: /ee/ spelt 'ie' ('diesel', 'hygiene', 'field', 'shield', 'brief', 'wield' and 'chief') and /ee/ spelt 'ei' after 'c' ('perceive', 'deceive' and 'conceive').

Answers

1. diesel		[example]
2. perceive		[1 mark]
3. hygiene		[1 mark]
4. field		[1 mark]
5. deceive		[1 mark]

6. shield [1 mark]

7. conceive [1 mark]

8. brief [1 mark]

9. wield [1 mark]

10. chief [1 mark]

Now try these

In this activity, children copy and complete sentences by choosing the correct spelling of each word. Reassure them that all the words fit the rule.

Answers

1. *The shopkeeper asked if they would like a receipt.* *[example]*

2. "Would you like a piece of cake?" asked Granny. [1 mark]

3. The pirates dug to retrieve the buried treasure. [1 mark]

4. The mayor is a pompous and conceited man. [1 mark]

5. Zofia received praise for her hard work. [1 mark]

6. The Amazons were fierce female warriors. [1 mark]

7. I am my uncle's favourite niece. [1 mark]

Support, embed & challenge

Support

Recap the /ee/ sound, invite the children to volunteer words with this sound, such as 'sleep', 'neat', 'cream', 'freeze' and 'ponies'. Write the words and underline the letters that stand for the /ee/ sound in each word. Use the examples to make a chart with the different spellings of /ee/ in each column. Provide these children with the word cards (see Additional resources) or cut out the words from Unit 7A Resource 1: Seize the ei spelling! Work with the children to locate the letters that stand for the /ee/ sound in each of these words. Sort the words into the two spelling patterns: 'ie' and 'ei'. Add examples of each spelling to the relevant columns of the chart. Display all the 'ei' words in the centre of the group. Put all the words in a bag and ask the children to take turns to draw a word and read it to the group. Challenge the rest of the group to say whether the word has an 'ie' or an 'ei' spelling.

Ask the children to complete Unit 7A Resource 1: Seize the ei spelling! (**Answers** /ee/ spelt 'ei' and coloured yellow: seize, conceive, conceited, receipt, either, caffeine, ceiling, deceive, receive)

Embed

Provide each child with a copy of Unit 7A Resource 1: Seize the ei spelling! Tell them to spend time learning the words, then to cut them out. Ask them to work in pairs to play a game of Snap. Tell the pairs to sit facing each other holding their cards. Each player simultaneously puts down one word at a time onto their pile set midway between the two players. They should keep putting words down on to their pile until a player spots a pair of words with a matching spelling of /ee/, at which point they should call 'Snap!' (This should happen often.) The player who called 'Snap!' must then cover the cards with their hands and spell both words. If the spelling is correct, they can gather up the words in the centre. The winner is the person with the most cards at the end.

Once the children are secure with these words, ask them to complete Unit 7A Resource 2: Let neither /ee/ spelling give you grief. (**Answers** chief, seize, believe, hygienic, conceited, fields, shield, piece, receipt, bunnies, either, grief, conceive, yield, caffeine, ceiling, deceive, brief, relieved, receive, achieve, niece, retrieve, deceitful, shriek, neither, perceive, cherries)

Challenge

Challenge these children to find as many words as they can with 'ceive' as a root (which has the meaning 'get'): 'receive', 'deceive', 'conceive', 'perceive', 'transceiver' and related words, such as 'receiver', 'deceived', 'preconceive', 'misperceived' and 'transceivers'.

Homework / Additional activities

Spelling test

Ask the children to learn one of the following lists of words for a spelling test. Challenge them to write sentences for five of the words on their list.

Core words	Support words	Challenge words
deceive	deceive	deceive
deceitful	deceitful	deceitful
undeceive	receive	undeceive
receive	receipt	receive
receipt	conceited	receipt
conceited	ceiling	conceited
misconceive	seize	misconceive
perceive	neither	perceive
ceiling	either	ceiling
seize	caffeine	seize
neither		neither
either		either
caffeine		caffeine
protein		protein
		receivers
		conceivable

Collins Connect: Unit 7

Ask the children to complete Unit 7 (see Teach → Year 5 → Spelling → Unit 7).

Unit 7B: Common words (3)

Overview

English curriculum objectives
- Word list – Years 5 and 6

Treasure House resources
- Spelling Skills Pupil Book 5, Unit 7B, pages 26–27
- Photocopiable Unit 7B, Resource 1: <u>Mischievous</u> spellings word search, page 96
- Photocopiable Unit 7B, Resource 2: Spelling <u>nuisance</u> words, page 97

Additional resources
- Word cards: soldier, thorough, stomach, shoulder, secretary, restaurant, queue, privilege, mischievous, parliament, persuade, neighbour, nuisance, definite, leisure, muscle
- Highlighters
- A bag to draw word cards from

Introduction

Teaching overview
This unit covers 16 more words from the list of words for Years 5 and 6: 'soldier', 'thorough', 'stomach', 'shoulder', 'secretary', 'restaurant', 'queue', 'privilege', 'mischievous', 'parliament', 'persuade', 'neighbour', 'nuisance', 'definite', 'leisure' and 'muscle'. Some of these words have 'silent' letters, such as the 'i' in 'soldier' and in 'nuisance', and some just have unusual spellings, such as 'shoulder'.

Introduce the concept
Organise the children into groups. Give each group of children a set of word cards and some highlighters (see Additional resources) and ask them to discuss in their groups what parts of these words they find particularly difficult to spell. For example, they may find the /ut/ sound spelt 'ite' at the end of 'definite' fairly tricky. Suggest that they swap the words between them, discussing ideas with a partner then feeding back to the group. Write all the words on the board and invite the groups to state which letters they think need to be remembered in each word. Discuss any that have a 'silent' letter that could be pronounced for spelling purposes, such as 'parl-i-ament', 'misch-i-e-vous' or 'rest-au-rant'.

Pupil practice

Pupil Book pages 26–27

Get started
In this activity, children write words and underline the parts of the words they find difficult to spell. Ask the children to read the words carefully and decide how the spelling is at odds with the pronunciation. Tell them that they do not all need to choose the same letters to underline if they find other letters tricky (for example, the 'd' in 'soldier').

Answers
Accept any underlining that indicates they understand the relationship between the spelling and the pronunciation.

1. soldi<u>e</u>r	[example]
2. th<u>orough</u>	[1 mark]
3. sh<u>ou</u>lder	[1 mark]
4. secreta<u>ry</u>	[1 mark]
5. rest<u>au</u>rant	[1 mark]
6. que<u>ue</u>	[1 mark]
7. privil<u>ege</u>	[1 mark]
8. mischi<u>evous</u>	[1 mark]

Try these
In this activity, children choose the correct spelling of each word. Give them time to look at the words in the introduction then tell them to cover the introduction and complete the activity.

Answers

1. parliament	[example]
2. persuade	[1 mark]
3. neighbour	[1 mark]
4. nuisance	[1 mark]
5. definite	[1 mark]
6. leisure	[1 mark]
7. muscle	[1 mark]

Now try these

In this activity, children copy and complete sentences, choosing the correct spellings of the missing words to fill the gaps.

Answers

1. *Can I persuade you to come swimming with me?*
[example]

2. Please give that dog a thorough rub down before he comes inside. [1 mark]

3. The queue was so long that Reuben missed the start of the film. [1 mark]

4. Mum will make a definite decision about the party tomorrow. [1 mark]

5. Uncle Jack has a medal from when he was a soldier. [1 mark]

Support, embed & challenge

Support

Practise reading the 16 words with the children. Read the word cards (see Additional resources), flashing them up until the children can read them fluently. Next, assign each child a word and ask him or her to be the expert in that word. Allow them all some time to memorise their word. Put all the words in a bag and take them out one at a time. Ask the expert to spell the word while the rest of the group write it on their whiteboards, following the expert's instructions. Repeat the exercise with two more words each.

Ask the children to complete Unit 7B Resource 1: Mischievous spellings word search. Afterwards, ask the children to tell you one of the words they were an expert in. See if they can remember the tricky part of their word.

Answers

m	u	s	c	l	e	q	g	g	a	s
a	j	b	w	e	q	g	o	h	j	e
w	d	e	f	i	n	i	t	e	d	c
h	v	h	m	s	x	m	a	z	y	r
c	e	x	n	u	i	s	a	n	c	e
m	f	b	g	r	s	o	n	b	m	t
q	u	e	u	e	h	l	k	p	z	a

y	o	y	g	o	c	d	s	z	e	r
j	s	d	k	f	l	i	f	v	n	y
p	r	i	v	i	l	e	g	e	k	n
x	d	f	k	r	y	r	v	m	c	k
n	e	i	g	h	b	o	u	r	v	e

Embed

Ask the children to write sentences for each word, combining words if helpful, to remind them of the spellings. For example: 'The secretary likes to tarry on her way to work; it's her little secret.' 'My stomach churns.' 'Ivan puts the i into mischievous.' 'Paul enjoys his jaunt at the restaurant.' 'Sue finds the queue goes on longer than she expects.' 'Our neighbour has a horse.'

Ask the children to complete Unit 7B Resource 2: Spelling nuisance words.

Challenge

These children have three words on their spelling list, 'definitely', 'persuaded' and 'thoroughly', where the suffixes '–ed' and '–ly' have been added to the tricky words. Challenge them to add other suffixes to other words on their spelling list and different suffixes to 'thorough', 'persuade' and 'definite'.

Homework / Additional activities

Spelling test

Ask the children to learn one of the following lists of words for a spelling test. Challenge them to write sentences for five of the words on their list.

Core and Support words		Challenge words	
soldier	mischievous	soldier	persuade
thorough	parliament	thorough	neighbour
stomach	persuade	stomach	nuisance
shoulder	neighbour	shoulder	definite
secretary	nuisance	secretary	leisure
restaurant	definite	restaurant	muscle
queue	leisure	queue	definitely
privilege	muscle	privilege	persuaded
		mischievous	thoroughly
		parliament	

Unit 8: The letter-string ough

Overview

English curriculum objectives
• Words containing the letter-string ough

Treasure House resources
• Spelling Skills Pupil Book 5, Unit 8, pages 28–29
• Collins Connect Treasure House Spelling Year 5, Unit 8
• Photocopiable Unit 8, Resource 1: Enough tough spellings!, page 98

• Photocopiable Unit 8, Resource 2: Thoroughly tough words, page 99

Additional resources
• Word cards: cough, trough, rough, tough, enough, plough, bough, drought, fought, brought, nought, thought, ought, bought, although, though, doughnut, thorough, borough, through

Introduction

Teaching overview

These words are often more confusing to read than they are to write, but the letter-string 'ough' is the cause of many spelling mistakes. It can be used to spell: /off/ as in 'cough' and 'trough'; /uff/ as in 'rough', 'tough' and 'enough'; /ow/ as in 'plough', 'bough' and 'drought'; /or/ as in 'fought', 'brought', 'nought', 'thought', 'ought' and 'bought'; /oa/ as in 'although', 'though' and 'doughnut'; /u/ as in 'thorough' and 'borough'; /ew/ as in 'through'. There is little logic to this spelling pattern and the words just need to be learned. There are about 20 of these words.

Introduce the concept

Organise the children into groups. Give each group of children a set of the word cards (see Additional resources). Ask them to read through the words together, deciding as a group on the correct pronunciation of each word. Ask the groups how many different pronunciations of 'ough' they have. (It should be seven.) Discuss the words as a class. Create a table on the board with the headings 'ough sounds /uff/', 'ough sounds /off/, 'ough sounds /ow/' 'ough sounds /or/' 'ough sounds /oa/' 'ough sounds /u/'and 'ough sounds /ew/'. Ask volunteers to add a word under each heading until the chart is complete.

Ask each group to nominate a scribe. Tell the children to work as a group to find a word from their set of word cards that rhymes with 'threw'. Tell the scribe to write the word on their whiteboard and hold it up. Repeat the exercise with 'stuff', 'off', 'cow', 'fort', 'toe' and 'horror'. Write the pairs of rhyming words on the board and ask a volunteer to underline the rhyming vowel.

Pupil practice

Pupil Book pages 28–29

Get started

In this activity, children sort words into three rhyming groups: words that rhyme with 'cow', with 'off' and with 'huff'. Practise reading the words on the list with the children, ensuring that they can all read them.

Establish that a 'bough' is an old-fashioned word for 'branch', a 'plough' is a series of metal blades on a long beam that breaks up the earth and a 'trough' is a large, low, drinking container for animals, or a low point in a wave motion.

Answers

Rhyme with 'cow'		Rhyme with 'off'		Rhyme with 'huff'	
bough	[example]	cough	[1 mark]	rough	[1 mark]
plough	[1 mark]	scoff	[1 mark]	tough	[1 mark]
bow	[1 mark]	trough	[1 mark]	stuff	[1 mark]
				enough	[1 mark]

Try these

In this activity, children write two words with the letter-string 'ough' to rhyme with each given word. Ask the children to attempt to complete the activity using their memory, but allowing them access to the word cards if they get stuck. Encourage them to add more words to each list if they know them.

Answers

Accept any two words with the letter-string 'ough' that rhyme with the given word.

1. *throw*	*although, dough*		*[example]*
2. caught	thought, bought		[2 marks]
3. scoff	trough, cough		[2 marks]
4. now	bough, plough		[2 marks]
5. know	dough, although		[2 marks]

Now try these

In this activity, children find and correct ten misspelt words in a paragraph. Read the text together, helping the children to spot the misspelt words before they write the words out correctly.

Answers

Althow *Although* it was sunny, the bitter cold made Saskia coff *cough*. But the wind was strong and Saskia thort *thought* it would be perfect for kite-flying. The string felt tuff *tough* in her hands as the kite tugged. Suddenly, a gust ruffly *roughly* wrenched the kite from her grasp. The kite dipped and swooped in whirls and troffs *toughs* until, suddenly, it plowed *ploughed* into a tall hedge and became stuck in the bow *bough* of a tree. "Oh no!" thort *thought* Saskia. "I'm not tall enuff *enough* to get it down from there!"

[9 marks, 1 mark for each correct answer]

Support, embed & challenge

Support

Focus with these children on the words 'cough', 'rough', 'tough', 'enough', 'fought', 'brought', 'bought', 'although', 'though' and 'through'. Read each word together, segmenting then blending each word. Cut up the word cards for these words (see Additional resources) into graphemes and recreate the words. Spend some time distinguishing between the meaning of 'bought' and 'brought'.

Ask the children to complete Unit 8 Resource 1: Enough tough spellings! If these children need further support, carry this out as a group activity before providing the children with individual copies. (**Answers** rhyming pairs: brought, bought and fought with sort, taught and fort; through with threw; tough and rough with puff and cuff; though and although with snow and low; enough with stuff; cough with off;1. bought, 2. brought, 3. enough)

Once the children are more confident with the spelling, ask them to take turns to remember one word with the 'ough' spelling. Challenge the rest of the group to write down the word, with your support if they need it.

Embed

Organise the children into groups and ensure each child has a whiteboard and pen. Tell the children

to take turns in their groups to make up sentences for 'brought' or 'bought', but say the word 'tomato' instead of 'brought' or 'bought' (or 'blank' if your children are in a riotous mood). The other children, without laughing, must write down the missing word. When they have all had a go, tell them to branch out to use other words that contain the 'ough' letter string.

Ask the children to complete Unit 8 Resource 2: Thoroughly tough words. (**Answers** cough, trough, rough, tough, enough, drought, brought, nought, thought, ought, bought, although, though, doughnut, thorough, borough; rough, through, fought, bough; 1. bought, 2. brought)

Challenge

Challenge these children to create a poster explaining the difference between 'bought' and 'brought'.

Ask these children to create exemplar sentences for a range of 'ough' words that can be used to challenge their classmates. Ask brave volunteers to read out their sentences, missing out the 'ough' word and challenge their classmates to write the missing word and hold it up.

Homework / Additional activities

Spelling test

Ask the children to learn one of the following lists of words for a spelling test. Challenge them to write sentences for five of the words on their list.

Core words	Support words	Challenge words
cough	cough	cough
rough	rough	rough
tough	tough	tough
enough	enough	enough
trough	plough	trough
bough	through	bough
plough	doughnut	plough
through	though	through
doughnut	although	doughnut
though	thorough	though
although	thought	although
thorough	bought	borough
thought	brought	thorough
bought		thought
brought		bought
drought		brought
		drought
		nought

Collins Connect: Unit 8

Ask the children to complete Unit 8 (see Teach → Year 5 → Spelling → Unit 8).

Unit 9A: Words with 'silent' letters

Overview

English curriculum objectives

- Words with 'silent' letters (i.e., letters whose presence cannot be predicted from the pronunciation of the word)

Treasure House resources

- Spelling Skills Pupil Book 5, Unit 9A, pages 30–31
- Collins Connect Treasure House Spelling Year 5, Unit 9
- Photocopiable Unit 9A, Resource 1: Sorting 'silent' letters, page 100

- Photocopiable Unit 9A, Resource 2: Subtle spellings, page 101

Additional resources

- Word cards: knee, knight, knuckle, knock, kneel, knot, wrapper, wrong, wrist, wreck, write, wrinkle, gnaw, gnash, gnome, gnarled, bomb, climb, thumb, lamb, plumber, limb, condemn, column, autumn, subtle, answer, island, stomach, receipt, doubt, rhythm, whale
- Poster paper and pens

Introduction

Teaching overview

Changes in pronunciation over the centuries have left the English language with many spellings that have redundant letters (not least those spelt 'ough'). Sounds have been dropped from the beginnings of words ('knight', 'gnome'), been lost from the ends ('climb', 'limb', 'solemn'), been lost from the middles ('subtle', 'salmon') and become indistinguishable from other sounds ('while', 'whale'). The result is some strange spellings and an increase in homophones ('whale' and 'wail', 'knot' and 'not', and so on).

Introduce the concept

Organise the children into small groups. Give each group a selection of the word cards (see Additional

resources). Ask them to read each word and decide what the spelling pattern is that you are practising this week. Ask each group to share their words with the next group and decide if they are correct in their assumption. Agree that you are looking at 'silent' letters and ask the children to underline the 'silent' letters in their words. Tell the children to write out their words on a whiteboard and agree in their groups how each word should be segmented (which grapheme will have the 'silent' letter). Write the words and segmentations on the board and see if you can find any helpful patterns (e.g., 'rh', 'wh', 'kn', 'gn' and 'mn').

Pupil practice

Pupil Book pages 30–31

Get started

In this activity, children sort words according to the 'silent' letter present in each of them. Ask the children to draw their own table and to use the words to fill

it in. Afterwards, draw a version on the board and ask the children to help you add a word or two to each column, for example, 'write', 'wrapper', 'knot', 'kneel', 'lamb', 'bomb'.

Answers

'Silent' 'w'		'Silent' 'k'		'Silent' 'b'	
wrapper	[1 mark]	knee	[example]	thumb	[1 mark]
wrong	[1 mark]	knight	[1 mark]	doubt	[1 mark]
wrist	[1 mark]	knuckle	[1 mark]		
wreck	[1 mark]	knock	[1 mark]		

Try these

In this activity, children choose the correct spelling of words with silent letters. Afterwards, add the new words from this activity to the chart on the board from the 'Get started' activity, adding a new column for a 'silent' 'n', 'g', 'l' and 'h'. Recap the fact that the 'l' is not really 'silent' in these letters: these are unusual spellings for /ar/ and /oa/.

Answers

1. *lamb*		*[example]*
2. column		[1 mark]
3. gnaw		[1 mark]
4. gnash		[1 mark]
5. calf		[1 mark]
6. autumn		[1 mark]
7. gnome		[1 mark]
8. rhythm		[1 mark]
9. folk		[1 mark]
10. gnarled		[1 mark]

Now try these

In this activity, children compose sentences for the target words 'lamb', 'column', 'gnaw', 'gnash', 'calf', 'autumn', 'gnome', 'rhythm', 'folk' and 'gnarled' (the words from the 'Try these' activity). Read the words together and ensure that the children understand the meaning of each word. Tell the children to share their ideas with a partner before writing. Afterwards, share the children's sentences.

Suggested answers

The lamb played in the field with its mother. [example]

Accept any sentences where the target word is correctly spelt and used.
[10 marks: 1 mark per sentence]

Support, embed & challenge

Support

Return to the word cards (see Additional resources) and read each one together. Write each word out and together segment the word, deciding which grapheme the 'silent' letter should be part of, for example, 'a-n-sw-er'. Underline each 'silent' letter and sort the cards into sets. Practise reading the words correctly.

Write the homophone pairs 'night' and 'knight', 'not' and 'knot', 'rapper' and 'wrapper', 'right' and 'write', 'nor' and 'gnaw', 'Ireland' and 'island', 'carves' and 'calves', 'Wales' and 'whales'. (If other children have already completed the Challenge task, ask them to give you their list of homophone pairs). Read the words together and underline the corresponding graphemes in each pair of words, discussing the difference in spelling. Ask each child in turn to choose a word for the group to practise spelling.

Ask the children to complete Unit 9A Resource 1: Sorting 'silent' letters. (**Answers** 'Silent' 'b': bomb, plumber, limb, subtle, climb, lamb, doubt, thumb; 'Silent' 'n': column, autumn, condemn; 'Silent' 'w': wrinkle, wrist, write, wrapper, wreck, answer, wrong; 'Silent' 'h': stomach, rhythm, whale; 'Silent' 'k': knight, knee, knock, kneel, knuckle, knot)

Embed

Ask the children to complete Unit 9A Resource 2: Subtle spellings. (**Answers** 1. write, 2. autumn,

3. subtle, 4. answer, 5. island, 6. plumber, 7. comb, 8. column, 9. stomach, 10. climb, 11. rhythm, 12. whale, 13. bombs, 14. salmon)

Once the children have carried out the activities in the Pupil Book and have completed the resource sheet, test their memory of words with 'silent' letters. Pin up six poster-sized pieces of paper around the classroom labelled 'silent k', 'silent w', 'silent b', 'silent g', 'silent h' and 'silent n'. Organise the children into six groups, one per poster. Give the groups about three minutes to write as many words as they can with the spelling pattern on their poster. Next, ask the groups to move round to the next sheet and add words that the previous group has missed. Repeat one more time so that each group has contributed to three sheets. Display the posters at the front of the classroom and add any additional words that you or the children can think of. Display the posters for the rest of the week.

Challenge

Ask these children to write a list of homophones to display alongside the lists made in the Embed activity. Challenge them to find homophones for 'night', 'not', 'rapper', 'right', 'nor', 'Ireland', 'carves' and 'Wales'.

Challenge the children to find five more words (with 'silent' letters) that have not been covered in this unit.

Homework / Additional activities

Spelling test

Ask the children to learn one of the following lists of words for a spelling test. Challenge them to write sentences for five of the words on their list.

Core words	Support words	Challenge words
limb	what	limb
comb	answer	comb
climb	island	climb
thumb	write	thumb
condemn	right	condemn
column	comb	solemn
solemn	climb	column
autumn	thumb	autumn
island	rhyme	island
subtle	stomach	stomach
wrinkle		subtle
receipt		wrinkle
rhyme		receipt
whale		rhyme
answer		whale
		answer
		knuckles
		wrestled

Collins Connect: Unit 9

Ask the children to complete Unit 9 (see Teach → Year 5 → Spelling → Unit 9).

Unit 9B: Common words (4)

Overview

English curriculum objectives
- Word list – Years 5 and 6

Treasure House resources
- Spelling Skills Pupil Book 5, Unit 9B, pages 32–33
- Photocopiable Unit 9B, Resource 1: Lightning crossword, page 102
- Photocopiable Unit 9B, Resource 2: Disastrous Snakes and Ladders, pages 103–104

Additional resources
- List of words: bruise, yacht, disastrous, category, bargain, vegetable, vehicle, sincerely, signature, awkward, twelfth, variety, physical, lightning, forty
- Counters and dice (for Resource 2)

Introduction

Teaching overview

This unit covers 15 more words from the list of words for Years 5 and 6. It includes words with 'silent' letters, words with missing letters and words that are just plain awkward! They are: 'bruise', 'yacht', 'disastrous', 'category', 'bargain', 'vegetable', 'vehicle', 'sincerely', 'signature', 'awkward', 'twelfth', 'variety', 'physical', 'lightning' and 'forty'.

Introduce the concept

Give each group of children a list of the 15 words covered in this unit (see Additional resources). Ask them to look at each word and mark the spelling pattern that they think they need to remember,

segmenting the words to see if that helps them with the spelling. Share the children's ideas, discussing the different issues with each word and segmenting the words where helpful. For example: in 'bruise', the /oo/ sound is spelt 'ui' and the /z/ sound is spelt 's'; 'yacht' just needs to be learned (if you want to own one someday) but the children might be interested to know that the 'ch' represents a missing /ch/ (as it also does in 'loch') as the original word was 'jachtschip', a Dutch word for a ship that chased pirates; 'disastrous' is easier with a northern accent and if we remember that /us/ at the end is spelt 'ous'; 'category' is easier to spell if we remember the related word 'categorise'. Some words lend themselves to overpronunciation, such as 'bargain' and 'vehicle'.

Pupil practice

Pupil Book pages 32–33

Get started

In this activity, children choose the correct spelling of each word. Afterwards, discuss which letters make these words difficult to spell. Talk about the difference between 'lightening' and 'lightning'.

Answers

1. *vehicle*	*[example]*
2. awkward	[1 mark]
3. yacht	[1 mark]
4. variety	[1 mark]
5. lightning	[1 mark]
6. signature	[1 mark]
7. sincerely	[1 mark]

Try these

In this activity, children correct the spellings of misspelt words. Tell the children to read the words in the introduction then cover them up and carry out the activity.

Answers

1. *physical*	*[example]*
2. twelfth	[1 mark]
3. disastrous	[1 mark]
4. bargain	[1 mark]
5. vegetable	[1 mark]
6. forty	[1 mark]
7. bruise	[1 mark]
8. category	[1 mark]

Now try these

In this activity, children compose sentences for the target words 'yacht', 'vehicle', 'awkward', 'forty', 'bargain', 'category', 'twelfth' and 'bruise'. Read the words together and ensure that the children understand the meaning of each word. Tell the children to share their ideas with a partner before writing. Afterwards, share the children's sentences.

Suggested answers

The millionaire threw a party aboard his enormous yacht.   *[example]*

Accept any sentences where the target word is correctly spelt and used.
[8 marks: 1 mark per sentence]

Support, embed & challenge

Support

Ask the children to complete Unit 9B Resource 1: Lightning crossword. (**Answers** across: 1. physical, 6. disastrous, 8. sincerely, 9. lightning; down: 2. yacht, 3. vehicle, 4. bruise, 5. bargain, 7. twelfth)

Return to the list of words for this unit (see Additional resources) and discuss how the children want to remember each word. Focus on the most useful words: 'bargain', 'lightning', 'vehicle', 'forty', 'disastrous' and 'vegetable'. Have the children take turns to choose a word for everyone to write on their whiteboard. Together, think of phrases to help remember the tricky spellings such as 'a bargain in the rain', 'the lightning **missed** me', 'his vehicle', 'disastrous for you not me', 'vege at the table'.

Use the game board on Unit 9B Resource 2: Disastrous Snakes and Ladders to play a game of Snakes and Ladders.

Embed

Once the children have had time to learn the words, ask them to use Unit 9B Resource 2: Disastrous Snakes and Ladders to play a game of Snakes and Ladders.

Provide the children with a list of the words from Unit 7B ('soldier', 'thorough', 'stomach', 'shoulder', 'secretary', 'restaurant', 'queue', 'privilege', 'mischievous', 'parliament', 'persuade', 'neighbour', 'nuisance', 'definite', 'leisure' and 'muscle') and from this unit and tell them to play a game of Hangman using them.

Challenge

Provide these children with some grid paper and ask them to create a word search using as many of the words from the Core and Support words spelling list (see Spelling test) as possible. Photocopy these for the rest of the class to solve.

Homework / Additional activities

Spelling test

Ask the children to learn one of the following lists of words for a spelling test. Challenge them to write sentences for five of the words on their list.

Core and Support words	Challenge words
bruise	bruise
yacht	bruising
disastrous	yacht
category	disastrous
bargain	category
vegetable	categorically
vehicle	bargain
sincerely	vegetable
signature	vehicle
awkward	sincerely
twelfth	signature
variety	awkward
physical	awkwardly
lightning	twelfth
forty	variety
	physical
	lightning
	forty

Review unit 2

Pupil Book pages 34–35

A. Children choose the correct spelling of each word.

Answers

1. necessary [1 mark]
2. queue [1 mark]
3. enough [1 mark]
4. yacht [1 mark]
5. cough [1 mark]
6. bruise [1 mark]
7. cooperate [1 mark]
8. rhythm [1 mark]
9. marvellous [1 mark]
10. awkward [1 mark]

B. Children look at the incorrectly spelt words and find the spelling mistake.
They then write the correct spelling.

Answers

1. thumb [1 mark]
2. re-enter [1 mark]
3. persuade [1 mark]
4. definite [1 mark]
5. thorough [1 mark]
6. receive [1 mark]
7. wreck [1 mark]
8. forty [1 mark]
9. occupy [1 mark]
10. de-ice [1 mark]

C. Children copy each sentence and complete the missing words.

Answers

1. Jill brought her PE kit to school. [1 mark]
2. Granny bought us an ice-cream. [1 mark]
3. Dad's chin is very rough and stubbly. [1 mark]
4. We went to the leisure centre to go swimming. [1 mark]
5. We hung streamers from the ceiling. [1 mark]

61

Unit 10A: Common words (5)

Overview

English curriculum objectives
- Word list – Years 5 and 6

Treasure House resources
- Spelling Skills Pupil Book 5, Unit 10A, pages 36–37
- Photocopiable Unit 10A, Resource 1: A 'conscious' or 'conscience' controversy, page 105
- Photocopiable Unit 10A, Resource 2: Playing with words, page 106

Additional resources
- Word cards: amateur, foreign, frequently, government, available, system, relevant, pronunciation, symbol, hindrance, conscience, conscious, desperate, controversy, convenience
- A bag to draw word cards from

Introduction

Teaching overview

This unit covers another 15 words from the list of words for Years 5 and 6: 'amateur', 'foreign', 'frequently', 'government', 'available', 'system', 'relevant', 'pronunciation', 'symbol', 'hindrance', 'conscience', 'conscious', 'desperate', 'controversy' and 'convenience'. Many of these are pretty tricky and not especially useful to Year 5 children – apart from the fact that they need to know them.

Introduce the concept

Organise the children into groups. Give each group a set of the word cards (see Additional resources) and ask them to discuss what they think each word means. Challenge them to write a definition on the back of as many of the cards as they can. ('Symbol' and 'system' are quite tricky to define.) Discuss the meaning of each word as a class. Give each group three words to focus on. Tell them to look at the

spellings and discuss which letters make the words tricky to spell. Ask them to compose a sentence for each of their three words. Share the children's ideas.

Talk about 'conscience' and 'conscious'. Look at the difference in the spellings and disambiguate the difference in meanings. Ask: 'Who has a conscience?' 'Do animals have consciences?' 'Could a robot ever be conscious?' 'What does it mean to be 'unconscious'?' Give examples of things that could cause a 'controversy' in your school, such as extending break or stopping PE.

Put the words in a bag and ask volunteers to take out a word at a time. Write each word on the board, describing the tricky spellings you need to remember as you write them.

Write 'disaster' and 'hinder' on the board, then 'disastrous' and 'hindrance'. Ask: 'How have the root words changed before the suffix was added?' Invite a volunteer to answer your question.

Pupil practice

Pupil Book pages 36–37

Get started

In this activity, children match words to their meanings. Discuss the meanings of the different words before asking the children to complete this activity, which covers the trickiest words.

Answers

1. *amateur*	*[example]*
2. controversy	[1 mark]
3. conscious	[1 mark]
4. conscience	[1 mark]
5. foreign	[1 mark]
6. hindrance	[1 mark]

Try these

In this activity, children write the correct spelling of each word. Once the children have had time to look at the words listed in the introduction, ask them to cover the opposite page in the Pupil Book and complete the activity. Check that they understand the meaning of each word, particularly 'controversy' and 'system'.

Answers

1. *available*	*[example]*
2. system	[1 mark]
3. symbol	[1 mark]
4. desperate	[1 mark]
5. relevant	[1 mark]

6. government   [1 mark]

7. controversy   [1 mark]

8. frequently   [1 mark]

Now try these

In this activity, children compose sentences for the target words 'amateur', 'conscience', 'hindrance', 'pronunciation' and 'convenience'. Read the words together and ensure that the children understand the meaning of each word. Tell the children to share their ideas with a partner before writing. Afterwards, share the children's sentences.

Suggested answers

Though only an amateur, William was an exceptional artist.   *[example]*

Accept any sentences where the target word is correctly spelt and used.
[5 marks: 1 mark per sentence]

Support, embed & challenge

Support

Many of these words will be tricky for these children, so focus on the words in their spelling list (see Spelling test) and spend time ensuring that the children are familiar with the words and their meanings.

Give a set of word cards for the words you are focusing on to each child (see Additional resources). Ask them to work in pairs to play a game of Pairs. This should increase their familiarity with the words and their ability to distinguish some of the more similar words from each other. Write the words out together and highlight the tricky parts of each word.

Embed

Ask the children to work in pairs and give each pair a set of word cards (see Additional resources). Ask them to work through the cards, practising the meaning of each word and using each word in a sentence. Tell them to say each word aloud and discuss which letters are tricky before taking it in turns to test one another on spelling the words. Tell the children to display the word cards between them and take turns to give each other spelling clues from which their partner must guess the word, for example: 'My third letter is 'n' and I have no 'e' in me.'

Ask them to complete Unit 10A Resource 1: A 'conscious' or 'conscience' controversy. Complete the sentences to practise the meaning of each word. (**Answers** 1. conscious, 2. unconscious, 3. conscience, 4. hindrance, 5. amateur, 6. controversy, 7. desperate, 8. system)

Challenge

Ask these children to complete Unit 10A Resource 2: Playing with words, which provides a slightly different context for the words and aims to increase their confidence with them. Warn the children that this resource sheet includes words from previous spelling tests. (**Answers** 1. frequently, 2. hindrance, 3. government, 4. pronunciation, 5. disastrous, 6. twelfth, 7. sincerely, 8. marvellous, 9. desperately, 10. immediately, 11. embarrassment, 12. awkwardly, 13. corresponding, 14. communication)

Ask these children to think of a short phrase for each word to act as an aide-memoire for the word's meaning, for example, 'unconscious mistake', 'heavy conscience', 'hindrance to success'.

Homework / Additional activities

Spelling test

Ask the children to learn one of the following lists of words for a spelling test. Challenge them to write sentences for five of the words on their list.

Core words	Support words	Challenge words
amateur	amateur	amateur
foreign	foreign	foreign
frequently	frequently	foreigner
government	available	frequently
available	system	government
system	relevant	available
relevant	symbol	system
pronunciation	conscience	relevant
symbol	conscious	pronounce
hindrance	desperate	pronunciation
conscience		symbol
conscious		hinder
desperate		hindrance
controversy		conscience
convenience		conscious
		desperate
		controversy
		convenience

Unit 10B: Homophones and near-homophones (1)

Overview

English curriculum objectives
- Homophones and other words that are often confused

Treasure House resources
- Spelling Skills Pupil Book 5, Unit 10B, pages 38–39
- Collins Connect Treasure House Spelling Year 5, Unit 10

- Photocopiable Unit 10B, Resource 1: Are you weary of spelling mistakes? page 107
- Photocopiable Unit 10B, Resource 2: Proceed to spell effectively, page 108

Additional resources
- Word cards: weary, wary, wearily, warily, proceed, precede, proceeds, precedes, affect, effect, effective, affected, desert, dessert
- Bags to draw word cards from

Introduction

Teaching overview

This unit covers four pairs of near-homophones: 'weary' (tired) and 'wary' (nervous); 'proceed' (continue), 'proceeds' (profit) and 'precede' (go before); 'affect' (influence) and 'effect' (consequence), 'desert' (desolate land) and 'dessert' (pudding). The trickiest of these are 'affect' (verb: to influence or make a difference to) and 'effect' (noun: the result or outcome).

Introduce the concept

Organise the children into groups. Give each group a set of word cards (see Additional resources) and ask them to sort them into homophones. Tell the children to race their classmates to pair up the homophones,

and decide on the meaning of each word. Ask each group to choose one or two pairs to explain to the class. Write the pairs on the board and discuss ways of remembering the different spellings, for example: 'dessert' has a double 's' because we always want seconds; 'desert' has a single 's' – you only want to go there once; in 'precede', the prefix 'pre' means 'before', as in 'previous'; 'proceed' means 'to go forward' as in 'progression'; 'effect' is a noun, as in 'special effect'; 'affect' is a verb so can be conjugated, as in 'affected' or 'affecting'; 'weary' – 'I fear you are weary dearie'; 'wary' – 'I am wary of scary things'. Ask the children for their own suggestions and encourage them to write down the ones they think will be useful.

Pupil practice

Pupil Book pages 38–39

Get started

In this activity, children match near-homophones to their definitions. Introduce the other meaning of 'desert' as in 'to leave behind in peril'.

Answers
1. desert   [example]
2. weary   [1 mark]
3. precede   [1 mark]
4. dessert   [1 mark]
5. wary   [1 mark]
6. effect   [1 mark]
7. affect   [1 mark]
8. proceed   [1 mark]

Try these

In this activity, children copy and complete the sentences by choosing the correct spelling of each missing word.

Answers
1. Chloe and Nick are learning how to make a dessert.   [example]
2. Long periods of bad weather can affect one's mood.   [1 mark]
3. It is very hot in the Sahara Desert.   [1 mark]
4. One should always be wary of crocodiles. [1 mark]
5. The horror film had disappointingly bad special effects.   [1 mark]
6. The adventurers were weary from travelling.   [1 mark]

Now try these

In this activity, children compose sentences for the target words 'wary', 'weary', 'desert', 'dessert', 'affect', 'effect', 'proceed', 'precede'. Read the words together and ensure that the children understand the meaning of each word. Tell the children to share their ideas with a partner before writing. Afterwards, share the children's sentences.

Suggested answers
You should always be wary of dragons. [example]

Accept any sentences where the target word is correctly spelt and used.
[8 marks: 1 mark per sentence]

Support, embed & challenge

Support

Ask the children to carry out Unit 10B Resource 1: Are you <u>weary</u> of spelling mistakes? This recaps on the meaning of each word. (**Answers** 1. proceeds, 2. desert, 3. effect, 4. weary, 5. precedes, 6. affect, 7. dessert, 8. wary)

Display the word cards between you (see Additional resources). Say one of the definitions from Resource 1 and ask the children to race to pick up the matching word card. When the children are confident with the meanings of the words, take away the cards and challenge the children to write the word on their whiteboards when you say the definition.

Embed

Ask the children to complete Unit 10B Resource 2: <u>Proceed</u> to spell <u>effectively</u>. (**Answers** 1. dessert, 2. affect, 3. desert, 4. effect, 5. wary, 6. wearily, 7. proceed, 8. precedes, 9. affected)

Once the children are confident of the meanings and spelling of each word, ask them to work in pairs and give each pair a set of word cards and a bag (see Additional resources). Tell them to take it in turns to pull one of the cards out of the bag and give their partner a clue to the word on the card, either by giving a definition, a cryptic clue or a sentence with a missing word. Their partner must then write down the word they think the clue is for.

Challenge

Provide these children with more practice on 'effect' and 'affect'. Ask them to investigate the meanings of the words, 'effectively', 'affectedness' and 'affectation'. Challenge them to fill the gaps in the following sentences. (The last one is very challenging.)

The icy pavement is _____ our ability to stand upright.   (affecting)

The sun and mist created a magical _____ on the water.   (effect)

Loom bands are banned from school, _____ immediately.   (effective)

The heavy rain _____ the driving conditions. (affected)

Eating a packet of sweets has _____ Anya's appetite. (affected)

The President has _____ changes that will negatively _____ the environment, _____ destroying the planet. (effected, affect, effectively)

Homework / Additional activities

Spelling test

Ask the children to learn the following sentences.

Ed was too weary after his swim to go to the park.
It is sensible to be wary of dogs you don't know.
Mr Davies gave the proceeds from the fair to charity.
Mum proceeded to tell us off when she saw the state of our bedrooms.
The preceding episode had ended on a cliffhanger.
The effect of the arrival of the headmaster was instant silence.
The arrival of the headmaster affects our behaviour.
The cactus is a desert plant.
My favourite dessert is chocolate sponge and custard.
Don't desert me here on my own.

Collins Connect: Unit 10

Ask the children to complete Unit 10 (see Teach → Year 5 → Spelling → Unit 10).

Unit 11: Homophones and near-homophones (2)

Overview

English curriculum objectives
- Homophones and other words that are often confused

Treasure House resources
- Spelling Skills Pupil Book 5, Unit 11, pages 40–41

- Collins Connect Treasure House Spelling Year 5, Unit 11
- Photocopiable Unit 11, Resource 1: Put spelling errors in the past, page 109
- Photocopiable Unit 11, Resource 2: A full complement of homophones, page 110

Introduction

Teaching overview

This unit covers four pairs of homophones: 'guessed' (the past tense of 'to guess') and 'guest' (a visitor); 'herd' (a collective noun for a group of animals) and 'heard' (the past tense of 'to hear'); 'past' (the time before now and also an adjective and preposition describing movement from one side to another) and 'passed' (the past tense of 'to pass'); 'led' (the past tense of 'to lead') and 'lead' (a soft heavy metal). The trickiest of these is the difference between 'passed' and 'past'. 'Passed' is always a verb, for example: 'We passed the shops.' 'The Tour de France passed through our village.' The verb in both these sentences is 'to pass'. All other parts of speech need 'past'. Confusion can arise when 'past' is used as an adverb, adjective or a preposition to describe a movement verb, for example: 'We drove past the shops.' 'The Tour de France has gone past our village.' 'It's past

three o'clock.' In these sentences, the verbs are 'to drive', 'to go' and 'to be'. The resource sheets attached to this unit provide practice of this.

Introduce the concept

Write the eight words on the board and ask volunteers to come to the front, pair up one pair of homophones and explain the difference between the two words. Continue until all the words are paired. Ask: 'How can we remember these words?' Aide-memoires could include: 'guessed' ends 'ed' because it is a past tense verb; a 'guest' stays in your house; 'herd' – 'the herd enter the field'; 'heard' – 'I heard with my ear'; 'passed' – 'we passed the house'; 'past' – 'last week is in the past' and 'last week we drove past the house'; 'lead' – 'too much lead is deadly'; 'led' – 'the path led to the shed'. Encourage the children to make their own suggestions and to write down the ones they think will be useful.

Pupil practice

Pupil Book pages 40–41

Get started

In this activity, children sort words into those spelt correctly and those spelt incorrectly and correct the words that are wrong.

Answers

Correct		Corrected	
herd	[example]	passed	[1 mark]
guest	[1 mark]	guest	[1 mark]
heard	[1 mark]	past	[1 mark]
past	[1 mark]	heard	[1 mark]
guessed	[1 mark]		
passed	[1 mark]		

Try these

In this activity, children sort words into their word type: 'nouns' or 'past tense verbs'. With the children, create a phrase for each of the words to clarify their meanings, for example: 'a herd of cows', 'I heard a

noise', 'an unexpected guest', 'past times', 'guessed the number', 'lead pencil', 'passed the book over', 'led out of assembly'. Discuss which words are verbs and which are nouns. Afterwards, ask which letter the past tense verbs end with. Ask: 'How will knowing this help your spelling?'

Answers

Nouns		Past tense verbs	
herd	[example]	heard	[1 mark]
guest	[1 mark]	guessed	[1 mark]
past	[1 mark]	passed	[1 mark]
lead	[1 mark]	led	[1 mark]

Now try these

Read the sentences together and ask the children to choose the correct spelling to complete each one. Then ask the children to copy and complete the sentences themselves.

Answers

1. *This morning, I heard my favourite song on the radio.* *[example]*

2. "May I sit?" asked Sam. "Be my guest!" replied Gale. [1 mark]

3. A herd of cows grazed peacefully in the field. [1 mark]

4. Captain Smith bravely led her troops to victory. [1 mark]

5. In the past, dinosaurs walked the Earth. [1 mark]

6. Lead is a soft, heavy metal that has many uses. [1 mark]

7. No one could have guessed what happened next. [1 mark]

8. It was too late; the moment had passed. [1 mark]

Support, embed & challenge

Support

Work with this group to create a table for the eight words and their meanings.

Ask the children to put the words 'hear', 'heard', 'lead', 'led', 'guess' and 'guessed' into verb pairs. Circle 'heard', 'led' and 'guessed' and ask the children to give you a homophone for each of these words.

Read these sentences to the children and ask them to write down the missing word.

The path through the trees _____ to a lonely lake.   (led)

The drainpipe was made of _____.   (lead)

Our tent was surrounded by a _____ of cows.   (herd)

Have you _____ anyone call us in for lunch?   (heard)

A _____ house is a type of hotel.   (guest)

Tom _____ the right number of sweets in the jar.   (guessed)

Felix zoomed _____ us on his scooter.   (past)

We _____ Felix in our car.   (passed)

Embed

Recap on the difference between 'past' and 'passed'. At first, clarify that 'the past' is any time before now.

Then move on to explain the difference between 'passed', the past participle of 'to pass', and 'past', a preposition that can explain movement. Help them to see why the spelling changes between: 'We passed John's house.' and 'We drove past John's house.' Ensure that the children can see that the verb in the first sentence is 'passed' and the verb in the second sentence is 'drove'. In the second sentence, 'past' describes where we drove.

Ask these children to complete Unit 11 Resource 1: Put spelling errors in the past. (**Answers** 1. past, 2. passed, 3. past, 4. past, 5. passed, 6. passed, 7. passed, 8. past, 9. past, 10. passed)

Challenge

Once these children are confident with the difference between 'passed' and 'past', ask them to investigate the definitions of and to practise using the homophones 'compliment' and 'complement', 'prophet' and 'profit', 'stationery' and 'stationary', 'symbol' and 'cymbal', 'desperate' and 'disparate'.

Ask the children to complete Unit 11 Resource 2: A full complement of homophones. (**Answers** 1. complemented, 2. profit, 3. symbols, 4. stationery, 5. complimented, 6. disparate, 7. cymbals, 8. prophet, 9. stationary, 10. desperate)

Homework / Additional activities

Spelling test

Ask the children to learn the following sentences.

Seb guessed what I was thinking.	Flynn passed his Grade 1 trombone exam.
We have a guest staying this weekend.	Hugh gave a cheery wave as he ran past me.
There is a herd of cows in the field.	We passed Ben's house on our way home.
Freya heard the ice-cream van outside.	Mrs Miles led the singing in assembly.
It's way past your bed time!	The lead in my pencil keeps breaking.

Collins Connect: Unit 11

Ask the children to complete Unit 11 (see Teach → Year 5 → Spelling → Unit 11).

Unit 12: Homophones and near-homophones (3)

Overview

English curriculum objectives

- Homophones and other words that are often confused

Treasure House resources

- Spelling Skills Pupil Book 5, Unit 12, pages 42–43
- Collins Connect Treasure House Spelling Year 5, Unit 12

- Photocopiable Unit 12, Resource 1: <u>Practising practice</u> and <u>practise</u>, page 111
- Photocopiable Unit 12, Resource 2: Higher homophones, page 112

Additional resources

- Word cards: licence, license, devise, device, advise, advice, practise, practice, prophecy, prophesy

Introduction

Teaching overview

This unit covers the following homophones and confusing words: 'licence' (noun: a piece of paper that gives you permission), 'license' (verb: to give permission), 'device' (noun: an appliance), 'devise' (verb: to create), 'advice' (noun: recommendation), 'advise' (verb: to recommend), 'practice' (noun: a custom, the act of trying to improve at something and a centre where a doctor or vet works), 'practise' (verb: to repeat for improvement, to carry out a custom). 'Licence', 'license', 'practice' and 'practise' are all homophones, whereas 'advice', 'advise', 'device', 'devise', 'prophecy' and 'prophesy' are near-homophones. In each case, the noun has the 'c' spelling and the verb the 's' spelling. The difference in pronunciation between 'advice' and 'advise' makes it the easiest pair to use correctly. Substituting 'advice' or 'advise' into sentences in place of any of the

homophones in this set can help indicate whether the context requires a verb or a noun (because only one will sound right).

Introduce the concept

Organise the children into groups. Hand out the word cards (see Additional resources), giving a set to each group of children. Ask them to put the words into their homophone pairs and then to decide how each is pronounced and which are homophones and which are near-homophones. Ask them to work out the difference between their pairs of words and challenge them to find a pattern. Ask: 'Which words are nouns and which are verbs?' Write the words on the board, explaining the differences between the words in each pair and providing examples of how to use them, such as 'a device for opening bottles', 'we need to devise a way to open bottles'.

Pupil practice

Pupil Book pages 42–43

Get started

In this activity, children sort words into two groups: nouns and verbs. After they have finished, ask them to look at the two lists and make a mental note of the spelling pattern: nouns end 'ce' and verbs end 'se'.

Answers

Nouns		Verbs	
practice	*[example]*	advise	[1 mark]
device	[1 mark]	license	[1 mark]
licence	[1 mark]	devise	[1 mark]
advice	[1 mark]	practise	[1 mark]

Try these

In this activity, children match words to their definitions. Remind the children of the work they did

in the 'Get started' activity. Recap on the fact that the nouns end 'ce' and the verbs end 'se'. Tell them to look out for clues in the definitions that point to a noun (the word 'a') or a verb (the word 'to').

Answers

1. *practice*		*[example]*
2. licence		[1 mark]
3. advice		[1 mark]
4. prophecy		[1 mark]
5. practise		[1 mark]
6. prophesy		[1 mark]
7. devise		[1 mark]
8. advise		[1 mark]
9. device		[1 mark]
10. license		[1 mark]

Now try these

In this activity, children copy and complete sentences using the appropriate words. Read the sentences with the children. Discuss what each missing word is and whether it is a verb or a noun.

Answers

1. *The doctor's advice was clear. "I advise you to stop putting things in your ears," he said.* [example]

2. "I can prophesy the future!" boasted the fortune-teller. "Cheapest prophecy for miles!" [2 marks]

3. The government plans to license the company to produce medicine. The licence will be issued next week. [2 marks]

4. These days, it is an uncommon practice among schoolchildren to practise standing up straight. [2 marks]

5. "I must devise a device to conquer the world," said the evil villain. [2 marks]

Support, embed & challenge

Support

Focus with these children on the most useful words in this unit, 'practice', 'practise', 'advice' and 'advise'. Start with the near-homophones 'advice' and 'advise'. Help the children to hear the difference between the two words, trying them out in different sentences, for example: 'The local advice is to keep off the ice.' 'My gran has given me nice advice twice.' 'Matt tries to advise me.' 'I'm advised not to eat all the pies.' Talk about the 'c' spelling of /s/ in words such as 'nice', 'mice', 'twice', 'slice' and the 's' spelling of /z/ as in 'rise', 'those' and 'these'. Move on to 'practice' and 'practise'. Explain that here the 'c' and the 's' both sound /s/ but the children should use their knowledge of 'advice' and 'advise' to remember which is the noun and which is the verb.

Ask the children to write 's' and 'c' on either side of their whiteboard. Read out a range of phrases using these words, including 'device' and 'devise', and ask the children to hold up 's' or 'c' to represent the spelling, for example, 'a handy device', 'please advise me', 'practise your spelling', 'the doctor's

practice', 'an explosive device', 'good advice', 'keep practising'.

Embed

Ask the children to complete Unit 12 Resource 1: Practising practice and practise. (**Answers** 1. licence, 2. licensed, 3. advice, 4. advised, 5. device, 6. devised, 7. Practice, 8. practises, 9. practice) Afterwards, ask them to compose their own sentences and ask a partner to check that they have used the words correctly.

Challenge

Ask these children to create a poster to help everyone remember the rules for this set of homophones.

Ask these children to learn the definitions for and to practise using the homophones 'hire' and 'higher', 'site' and 'sight', 'bored' and 'board', 'pore' and 'poor', 'waste' and 'waist'.

Ask the children to complete Unit 12 Resource 2: Higher homophones. (**Answers** 1. pore, 2. bored, 3. higher, 4. sight, 5. hire, 6. poor, 7. waist, 8. site, 9. board, 10. waste)

Homework / Additional activities

Spelling test

Ask the children to learn the following sentences.

> Auntie Elaine has her pilot's licence.
>
> We were licensed to drive the car on holiday.
>
> We needed to devise a cunning escape plan.
>
> This clever device will turn you invisible.
>
> I would not advise you to go up the mountain in this weather.
>
> My advice would be to take a waterproof.
>
> Make sure you practise your spellings.
>
> Hockey practice is on Thursday this week.

Collins Connect: Unit 12

Ask the children to complete Unit 12 (see Teach → Year 5 → Spelling → Unit 12).

Unit 13: Homophones and near-homophones (4)

Overview

English curriculum objectives
- Homophones and other words that are often confused

Treasure House resources
- Spelling Skills Pupil Book 5, Unit 13, pages 44–45
- Collins Connect Treasure House Spelling Year 5, Unit 13

- Photocopiable Unit 13, Resource 1: Homophone crossword, page 113
- Photocopiable Unit 13, Resource 2: A short <u>course</u> in more homophones, page 114

Additional resources
- Word cards: serial, cereal, aisle, isle, aloud, allowed, draught, draft, principal, principle, stationary, stationery

Introduction

Teaching overview
This unit covers six pairs of homophones: 'aisle' (a gap between seats or shelves), 'isle' (an island), 'serial' (a series of stories about the same characters; something that happens again and again), 'cereal' (a breakfast food; wheat, corn or barley), 'aloud' (out loud), 'allowed' (given permission), 'draft' (a rough version of a piece of work), 'draught' (a breeze inside a building), 'principal' (main), 'principle' (a theory or belief), 'stationary' (not moving), 'stationery' (pens, pencils, envelopes, paper, and so on).

Introduce the concept
Ask the children to work in pairs. Assign each pair of children a pair of homophones and give them the relevant word cards (see Additional resources). Ask them to read their words and decide what each one means. Challenge them to write a definition for each word on the back of the cards. Ask the pairs of children to get into groups according to the

homophone pairs they were assigned (so there are six groups, each working on a homophone pair). Ask the pairs in the groups to compare the definitions they wrote and to improve their definitions if they can. Invite volunteers from each group to write their words, with definitions, on the board. Discuss the words together, focusing on those words that are a bit more challenging in meaning or spelling, such as 'draught', 'aisle', 'isle', 'principal' and 'principle'. Work together to create aide-memoires for each word, such as: 'the aisle of the train'; 'isle' is short for 'island'; 'a serial is a series'; 'cereal is crunchy and really healthy'; 'aloud' is 'out loud'; 'allowed' ends 'ed' because it is a past tense verb; 'the first draft was daft so I rewrote it'; 'we were caught in a draught'; 'my best pal is my principal pal'; 'I have triple chocolate sauce on my ice-cream on principle'; pens, pencils and envelopes are types of stationery; 'stationary' means 'standstill'. Share the ideas, encourage the children to think of their own and tell them to write down the phrases that they think will be most useful.

Pupil practice
Pupil Book pages 44–45

Get started
In this activity, children choose the correct spelling of each word.

Answers
1. *serial*	[example]
2. aisle	[1 mark]
3. aloud	[1 mark]
4. draught	[1 mark]
5. principal	[1 mark]
6. cereal	[1 mark]
7. isle	[1 mark]
8. draft	[1 mark]
9. allowed	[1 mark]
10. principle	[1 mark]

Try these
In this activity, children match words to their definitions.

Answers
1. *stationery*	[example]
2. cereal	[1 mark]
3. draft	[1 mark]
4. serial	[1 mark]
5. draught	[1 mark]
6. stationary	[1 mark]
7. principal	[1 mark]
8. principle	[1 mark]

Now try these

In this activity, children copy and complete the sentences by choosing the correct spelling of each missing word.

Answers

1. *Mandeep enjoyed the new three-part drama serial, 'Pirates'.* *[example]*

2. Pencils, erasers and rulers are all items of stationery. [1 mark]

3. The cars in the traffic jam had been stationary for hours. [1 mark]

4. Carl is not allowed to go to the match this weekend. [1 mark]

5. We have to write the first draft of the essay by Monday. [1 mark]

6. Ava eats a bowl of cereal every day before school. [1 mark]

7. An icy draught blew through the neglected castle. [1 mark]

Support, embed & challenge

Support

Focus on the words 'aloud', 'allowed', 'draft', 'draught', 'cereal' and 'serial' with these children. Practise spelling the words together and clarify the different meanings. Ask the children to work in pairs and give each pair a set of words cards for the words you are focusing on (see Additional resources). Have the children place the cards equidistantly between them. Say a sentence, emphasising the target word, and ask the children in each pair to race each other to touch the card with the correct spelling.

Work through Unit 13 Resource 1: Homophone crossword as a group exercise. (**Answers** across: 2. principle, 5. isle, 7. draft, 8. aloud; down: 1. aisle, 3. cereal, 4. principal, 6. serial)

Embed

Organise the children into groups of six and provide each group with a set of word cards (see Additional resources). Tell them to each take two words (ensuring they do not have two homophones) and to display them in front of themselves. Tell one child in each group to think of a sentence for one of someone else's words. The child whose word it is must say 'mine' and pick up the word before another member of the group says their name. The person who first says 'mine' or the child's name gets a point. The person whose word it was makes up the next sentence. (Encourage the children to ensure each child in the group is picked equally.)

Ask the children to complete Unit 13 Resource 1: Homophone crossword. If they are very confident with the words, delete the words at the bottom of the page before photocopying the worksheet. (**Answers** see above)

Challenge

Once the children are confident with the words for this unit, ask them to find out the meanings of and to practise spelling the homophones: 'bite' and 'byte', 'caught' and 'court', 'course' and 'coarse', 'currant' and 'current', 'laps' and 'lapse'. Once they understand the words, ask them to complete Unit 13 Resource 2: A short course in more homophones. (**Answers** 1. course, 2. current, 3. byte, 4. caught, 5. coarse, 6. bite, 7. laps, 8. currant, 9. court, 10. lapse)

Homework / Additional activities

Spelling test

Ask the children to learn the following sentences.

Do not leave your bags in the aisle.	May I remind you that you are not allowed on the grass?
The Summer Isles are off the coast of Scotland.	
The serial on the television finished on a cliffhanger each week.	Tilly read the rough draft of my story.
	I felt chilly sitting in the draught by the door.
Corn, wheat and barley are types of cereal.	I don't eat meat on principle.
Polly read her poem aloud in assembly.	The Queen's principal residence is Buckingham Palace.

Collins Connect: Unit 13

Ask the children to complete Unit 13 (see Teach → Year 5 → Spelling → Unit 13).

Unit 14: Homophones and near-homophones (5)

Introduction

Teaching overview

This last unit covers the homophones 'mourning' (grieving from loss), 'morning' (beginning of the day), 'ascent' (journey upwards), 'assent' (agreement), 'bridle' (straps around a beast's head for controlling it), 'bridal' (to do with a bride), 'descent' (journey down), 'decent' (pretty good or morally correct), 'dissent' (disagreement), 'father' (male parent), 'farther' (longer distance), 'steel' (type of metal), 'steal' (take something that is not yours without permission), 'whose' (belonging to whom) and 'who's' (contraction of 'who is' or 'who has').

Introduce the concept

Organise the children into groups. Hand out a set of word cards (see Additional resources) to each group and ask them to put them into their homophone pairs. (Warn them that there is one trio.) Tell them to discuss the meaning of each word, making notes

on the back of the cards when they feel confident. Discuss the trio of words, pointing out that 'decent' is not quite a homophone (it is not pronounced exactly like 'dissent' or 'descent') but the similarities between the three words could be confusing.

Share all the words and the children's definitions, creating a list on the board. Clarify the meanings of any words the children did not recognise, giving examples of usage. Pair the antonyms 'descent' and 'ascent' and 'dissent' and 'assent'. Point out the patterns in the spellings. Provide examples of these words in use, for example: 'The steep descent was rather scary.' 'Jess's ascent of the climbing wall was fast.' 'There was grumbling and dissent when Mum suggested a walk in the countryside.' 'If everyone gives their assent, I'll buy the tickets now'. Assign each group one of the words and ask them to compose a sentence using their word. When they have had time to do so, invite each group to share their sentence.

Pupil practice

Pupil Book pages 46–47

Get started

In this activity, children identify and write the correctly spelt words in sets of correctly and incorrectly spelt words. Clarify the meaning of each word.

Answers

1. *ascent, assent*		[example]
2. descent		[1 mark]
3. morning, mourning		[2 marks]
4. steal, steel		[2 marks]
5. who's, whose		[2 marks]
6. dissent		[1 mark]
'Who's' is a contraction of two words.		[1 mark]

Try these

In this activity, children match words to their definitions.

Answers

1. *dissent*		[example]
2. bridle		[1 mark]
3. farther		[1 mark]
4. mourning		[1 mark]
5. father		[1 mark]
6. steal		[1 mark]
7. descent		[1 mark]
8. steel		[1 mark]
9. morning		[1 mark]
10. bridal		[1 mark]

Now try these

In this activity, children copy and complete the sentences by choosing the correct spelling of each missing word.

Answers

1. *The walkers were glad the <u>descent</u> from the mountains was over.* *[example]*

2. The mayor, <u>whose</u> face was bright red, spluttered with rage. [1 mark]

3. The teachers were all in <u>assent</u> that the trip should proceed. [1 mark]

4. "<u>Who's</u> there?" asked the night watchman. "Show yourself!" [1 mark]

Support, embed & challenge

Support

Work with these children on the most useful homophone pair in this set: 'who's' and 'whose'. Ask them to write 'whose' on one side of their whiteboards and 'who's' on the other. Read out sentences that use these words and ask the children to hold up the correct word for each sentence. Remind them that, if they are not sure, they should try replacing 'who's'/'whose' with 'who is' or 'who has'. If neither replacement works, then the word is 'whose'. If necessary, talk about each example in turn, discussing the meaning of the words in each context. Sentences could include: 'Who's coming to dinner?' 'Whose are these shoes?' 'The man whose car that is lives next door.' 'Who's borrowed the scissors and not put them back?' 'Jan, who's this week's golden child, is always polite.' 'There's the lady whose son plays rugby with Cameron.'

Embed

Organise the children into groups of five and provide each group with a set of word cards (see Additional resources). Tell them to each take three words (ensuring they do not have two homophones) and to display them in front of themselves. Tell one child in each group to think of a sentence for one of someone else's words. The child whose word it is must say 'mine' and pick up the word before another member of the group says their name. The person who first says 'mine' or the child's name gets a point. The person whose word it was makes up the next sentence. (Encourage the children to ensure each child in the group is picked equally.)

Ask the children to complete Unit 14 Resource 1: <u>Who's decent</u> at spelling? If they are very confident with the words, delete the words at the bottom of the page before photocopying the worksheet. (**Answers** 1. steel, 2. descent, 3. mourning, 4. father, decent, 5. whose, 6. dissent, 7. farther, 8. bridal, 9. assent, 10. steal)

Challenge

Once the children are confident with the words for this unit, ask them to find out the meanings of and to practise spelling the homophones: 'praise', 'prays' and 'preys'; 'peek', 'peak' and 'pique'; 'thrown' and 'throne'; 'sweet' and 'suite'; 'stake' and 'steak'.

Ask the children to complete Unit 14 Resource 2: Homophones: There's meaning at <u>stake</u>. (**Answers** 1. praise, 2. prays, 3. preys, 4. sweet, 5. peak, 6. pique, 7. throne, 8. thrown, 9. suite, 10. stake, 11. steak)

Homework / Additional activities

Spelling test

Ask the children to learn the following sentences.

The first ascent of Mount Everest was in 1953.	Let's steal away while she's not looking.
I hope Mum assents to the sleepover.	The steel girders were very strong.
The steep descent was hard on the knees.	Who's been eating my porridge?
The dissenters in the party all refused to walk back.	Whose turn is it to go first?
You need a decent night's sleep.	Keep walking; it's not much farther.
Good morning! Time to get up.	The bridal car is waiting outside the church.
Granny is mourning the loss of her cat who died last week.	The horse's bridle jingled as he trotted along.

Collins Connect: Unit 14

Ask the children to complete Unit 14 (see Teach → Year 5 → Spelling → Unit 14).

Review unit 3

A. Children look at the incorrectly spelt words and find the spelling mistake. They then write the correct spelling.

Answers

1. amateur [1 mark]
2. foreign [1 mark]
3. government [1 mark]
4. conscious [1 mark]
5. desperate [1 mark]
6. controversy [1 mark]
7. conscience [1 mark]
8. hindrance [1 mark]
9. symbol [1 mark]
10. relevant [1 mark]

B. Children copy and complete each sentence by adding the missing letter or letters to the bold words.

Answers

1. Let's **practise** our dance. [1 mark]
2. That was a very short piano **practice**. [1 mark]
3. The man at the pet shop gave us lots of **advice**. [1 mark]
4. I'd **advise** you to go out before it rains. [1 mark]
5. We bought a fishing **licence**. [1 mark]
6. I did not **license** you to go crazy. [1 mark]
7. The sunshine had a bad **effect** on the snowman. [1 mark]
8. Kevin's stomach ache **affected** his performance. [1 mark]
9. Fergus walked slowly and **warily** over the swaying, rope bridge. [1 mark]
10. It was a long, hot drive across the **desert**. [1 mark]

C. Children copy and complete each definition by writing the missing letters for the key word.

Answers

1. To go forwards is to 'proceed'. [1 mark]
2. To go before is to 'precede'. [1 mark]
3. A flow of air inside a building is a 'draught'. [1 mark]
4. The past tense of 'guess' is 'guessed'. [1 mark]
5. The main or most important thing is the 'principal'. [1 mark]
6. 'Whose' means 'belonging to whom'. [1 mark]
7. 'Farther' means 'greater distance'. [1 mark]
8. The journey down something is called the 'descent'. [1 mark]
9. Pens, pencils and rulers are types of 'stationery'. [1 mark]
10. A space between rows of chairs is called an 'aisle'. [1 mark]

Ambi<u>tious</u> adjectives

Look at these words. Match the related adjectives and nouns and write them at the bottom as pairs. One has been done for you.

space	nutritious	delicacy
grace	ambition	ferocity
spacious	cautious	vicious
gracious	infectious	ferocious
infection	vice	caution
nutrition	ambitious	delicious
anxious	anxiety	

Noun   **Adjective**

space _____   *spacious* _____

_____   _____

_____   _____

_____   _____

_____   _____

_____   _____

_____   _____

_____   _____

Don't be anx<u>ious</u> about spelling

Choose the correct spellings of these words.
Write each correct word on its answer line.

1.   spacious   spatious   _____

2.   nutricious   nutritious   _____

3.   precious   pretious   _____

4.   ferocious   ferotious   _____

5.   caucious   cautious   _____

6.   infecious   infectious   _____

7.   anxious   antious   _____

8.   delicious   delitious   _____

Use the words from above to complete these noun phrases. Look at the words in brackets for clues to which word to use.

1.   an _____ mother at the skate park   (worried)

2.   a _____ but disgusting smoothie   (healthy)

3.   a _____ tiger defending her cubs   (fierce)

4.   a _____ cake covered in cherries   (tasty)

5.   a _____ tight rope walker   (careful)

6.   an _____ disease   (catching)

7.   my mother's _____ diamond ring   (valuable)

8.   a _____ house in the country   (roomy)

An unofficial outing

Find all the words in the story that end **–cial** or **–tial**.
Write each word in the correct column of the table
below the story.

It was Sophie's unofficial birthday. Sophie's real birthday was in November but she often had her special outing in the middle of summer when there was less chance of torrential rain. When Dad suggested going canoeing, Sophie's initial reaction was "Oh, no!" Anything to do with water did not sound to Sophie as if it had the potential for fun.

They arrived at the artificial lake and a guide provided them with a canoe and life jackets. He talked enthusiastically to Sophie's dad about how beneficial water sports are for our health. Sophie didn't care about the health benefits. Sophie was just worried about falling in. The water looked glacial. Okay, it was the middle of summer. But it was the middle of summer in Scotland…

They canoed out to a small island in the middle of the lake and pulled their boats ashore. Dad produced a substantial picnic from his bag, complete with the crucial birthday cake! They sat in the partial shade of a tree and ate and chatted. It was heaven. Maybe canoeing isn't so bad after all, Sophie thought. They still had to canoe back, though.

/shul/ spelt **cial**	/shul/ spelt **tial**

Essential words, beneficial spellings

Choose the correct spellings of the words.
Write each correct word on its answer line.

1. official   offitial   _____

2. antisocial   antisotial   _____

3. essencial   essential   _____

4. beneficial   benefitial   _____

5. marcial   martial   _____

6. artificial   artifitial   _____

7. inicial   initial   _____

8. influencial   influential   _____

9. confidencial   confidential   _____

10. substancial   substantial   _____

Use the words above to complete the sentences. Look at the words in brackets for clues to which word to use.

1. Screaming loudly in shops is _____.   (inconsiderate)

2. I wouldn't have guessed the flowers were _____.   (fake)

3. This conversation is _____: it's just you and me.   (private)

4. It's _____ that you check the brakes on your bike regularly.   (important)

5. The _____ payment for the trip will be £5.   (first)

6. _____ arts training can teach you self-control.   (combat)

7. I'm offering a _____ reward for finding my missing cat.   (big)

8. Wear your school uniform for _____ class photos on Friday.   (authorised)

9. A varied diet is _____ to one's health.   (advantageous)

10. The President is one of the most _____ people in the world.   (significant)

Import<u>ant</u> spellings for intellig<u>ent</u> stud<u>ents</u>

1. Colour all the words that end **–ent** yellow and all the words that end **–ant** green.

parent	experiment	brilliant	different
distant	elegant	accident	hesitant
agreement	argument	instant	pleasant
relevant	reluctant	excellent	significant
innocent	tyrant	movement	elephant
constant	competent	present	vacant
student	important	treatment	arrogant
infant	equipment	comment	intelligent
extravagant	content	triumphant	silent
settlement	assistant	frequent	servant

2. Use this grid to play a game with a partner. Your teacher will tell you what to do.

Relevant words, significant sentences

Read the words at the bottom of the page. Practise
spelling them. Fold the words away to hide them.

Use the words to complete the sentences. Look at the words in brackets for clues.

Can you remember which words end **–ent** and which end **–ant**?

1. Ross looked through his telescope at the _____ stars and planets.   (far)

2. My little sister looks _____ but she is really very naughty.   (guiltless)

3. It is _____ to eat five portions of fruit or vegetables a day.   (crucial)

4. There was an _____ "Ring, ring, ring!" on the doorbell.   (pressing)

5. "Only the _____ details please, madam," said the constable,
    wearily.   (related)

6. Evie and Grace are twins but they look quite _____.   (dissimilar)

7. I'm so sorry! It was an _____!   (mishap)

8. The new head teacher has made _____
    changes to our school.   (major)

9. Thank you, Richard. That was an _____ story.   (fantastic)

10. There are two species of _____: African and
    Asian.   (pachyderm)

11. Our dog is not very _____ and she doesn't
    come when called.   (biddable)

------------------------------ fold here -------------------------------

distant   elephant   important   significant   relevant   different   obedient
accident   excellent   urgent   innocent

Spell with confid<u>ence</u>

Pair up these words and use them to fill in the table.

distance	expectancy	urgent	infant
elegance	observant	intelligence	elegant
observance	magnificence	infancy	urgency
efficient	intelligent	independence	magnificent
expectant	distant	efficiency	independent

Adjectives (ending –ant or –ent)	Nouns (ending –ance, –ency, –ence or –ency)
fluent	fluency

Spell with compet<u>ency</u>

Fill in the missing words in this table. Watch out: not all the words exist. If there isn't a word for a space, just write 'no word'.

Adjective (ending **–ant** or **–ent**)	Noun (ending **–ance**, **–ency**, **–ence** or **–ency**)
(no word)	disturbance
efficient	
	experience
consequent	
violent	
	sentence
elegant	
	appearance
	coincidence
expectant	
decent	
	intelligence
confident	
magnificent	
	ignorance
infant	

Appreciate these excellent words!

Write these words in the grids. Write one sound in each box.

1. accompany

2. according

3. attached

4. committee

5. community

6. correspond

7. embarrass

8. apparent

Now write each of these words in the same style in your notebook.

accommodate   exaggerate

aggressive   excellent

appreciate   immediate

communicate

Excellent words to communicate with

Can you remember these spellings? Read the word out loud.
Check which letters are doubled and which are not. Cover
the word, write it in the next column then uncover the word to check
the spelling. Do this again, two more times.

Read the word	Write the word	Write the word	Write the word
accommodate			
accompany			
according			
aggressive			
apparent			
appreciate			
attached			
committee			
communicate			
community			
correspond			
embarrass			
exaggerate			
excellent			
immediate			

Are you <u>able</u> to add <u>ible</u> and <u>able</u>?

Add **ible** or **able** to these roots.

Remember:

* If you're **able** to see a complete word, add **able**.

* If a whole word is impos**sible** to see, add **ible**.

reason_____   horr_____

incred_____   comfort_____

remark_____   terr_____

respons_____   accept_____

miser_____   invis_____

defens_____   pay_____

suit_____   imposs_____

notice_____   profit_____

Sort the words into the correct list.

Words ending **ible**	Words ending **able**

Sensible words spelt predictably

Choose the correct spellings of these words. Write each correct word on its answer line.

flexibly	flexably	_____
forcibly	forcably	_____
inevitibly	inevitably	_____
remarkibly	remarkably	_____
terribly	terrably	_____
comfortibly	comfortably	_____
suitibly	suitably	_____
incredibly	incredably	_____
sensibly	sensably	_____
arguibly	arguably	_____
understandibly	understandably	_____
visibly	visably	_____
uncomfortibly	uncomfortably	_____
impossibly	impossably	_____
noticeibly	noticeably	_____
horribly	horrably	_____
miseribly	miserably	_____
responsibly	responsably	_____
predictibly	predictably	_____
forcibly	forcably	_____
improbibly	improbably	_____
memoribly	memorably	_____

Suffering from stress

- Underline the strongest stress in each word.

- Colour in red the words with a double **r** in the middle.

- Colour in yellow the words with a single **r** in the middle.

suffering	buffer	buffering
inferring	offered	preferring
differing	preference	proffer
inference	pilfering	offering
suffered	referee	transferring
preferred	transferred	pilfer
difference	proffered	referral

Can you hear the <u>difference</u>?

Add **–ed**, **–ing** and **–ence** to the root words. Remember to say each word aloud and listen carefully to decide if you need one r or two. Write each word in the table.

Verb	Add –ed	Add –ing	Add –ence
defer			
refer			
differ			
confer			
transfer			
infer			
prefer			

Marvellous words to occupy you

Write the words in the grids. Write one sound in each box.
The first one has been done for you.

1. immediately

i	mm	e	d	i	a	t	e	l	y

2. interrupt

3. necessary

4. occupy

5. opportunity

6. programme

7. suggest

8. marvellous

An <u>opportunity</u> to learn <u>necessary</u> spellings

Cut out these cards and place them face down. Take turns with a partner to turn over two cards. If the turned-over pair have the same double letter (shown in bold), that player keeps the pair.

a**cc**ording	a**cc**ompany	a**pp**arent	a**pp**reciate
i**mm**ediate	co**mm**unity	co**mm**ittee	co**mm**unicate
co**rr**espond	inte**rr**upt	embarra**ss**	nece**ss**ary
exa**gg**erate	su**gg**est	exce**ll**ent	marve**ll**ous
i**mm**ediately	progra**mm**e	o**cc**upy	o**cc**ur
profe**ss**ion	aggre**ss**ive	reco**mm**end	acco**mm**odate

Re-examining hyphens

Read these words and decide whether they should have hyphens or not.

Cross out the words that are wrong and write them with a hyphen.

Remember, the word needs a hyphen if:

- the prefix ends with the same letter as the word starts with (for example, c**o**-**o**wn)

- the prefix is **anti–** or **ex–** (for example, **anti**-aging, **ex**-soldier).

reexamine	_____	expresident	_____
remember	_____	reenter	_____
coopt	_____	recover	_____
unkind	_____	reeducate	_____
reenact	_____	reheat	_____
reenforce	_____	reevaluate	_____
coown	_____	unpack	_____
coauthor	_____	reexplain	_____
preelection	_____	return	_____
defrost	_____		

Re-enforcing good hyphenation

Read these words and decide whether they should have hyphens or not. Cross out the words that are wrong and write them with a hyphen.

Remember, the word needs a hyphen if:

- the prefix ends with the same letter as the word starts with (for example, c**o-o**wn)

- the prefix is **anti–** or **ex–** (for example, **anti**-aging, **ex**-soldier)

- if the new word looks peculiar without a hyphen (for example, **coworker**).

Remember, we don't need a hyphen if:

- the prefix and root create a very common word (for example, **reassure**).

antivenom	_____	recollect	_____
coauthor	_____	recover	_____
coeducation	_____	reenact	_____
costar	_____	reenergise	_____
deice	_____	reenforce	_____
nonstop	_____	reenter	_____
copilot	_____	nonsense	_____
cooperate	_____	reevaluate	_____
coordinate	_____	reexplain	_____
nonstick	_____	reheat	_____
coincidence	_____	icecream	_____
coopt	_____	remember	_____
coown	_____	return	_____
reappear	_____	reexamine	_____
expresident	_____	unkind	_____
reassure	_____	preelection	_____
reeducate	_____	unpack	_____

Seize the ei spelling!

1. Find all the words in this chart with the /ee/ sound spelt **ei** and colour them yellow.

chief	seize	believe	hygienic	conceive
mischief	conceited	fields	shield	piece
receipt	bunnies	either	grief	yield
caffeine	field	ceiling	shield	deceive
brief	relieved	receive	achieve	niece

2. Use these cards to play a game of Snap.

Let n<u>ei</u>ther /ee/ spelling give you gr<u>ie</u>f

All these words have a missing /ee/ sound. Write **ie** or **ei** to complete the words correctly.

ch____f

s____ze

bel___ve

hyg____nic

conc____ted

f____lds

sh____ld

p____ce

rec____pt

bunn____s

____ther

gr____f

conc___ve

y____ld

caff____ne

c____ling

dec____ve

br____f

rel____ved

rec____ve

ach____ve

n____ce

retr____ve

dec____tful

shr____k

n____ther

perc____ve

cherr____s

Mischievous spellings word search

Find these words in the word search.

> privilege   neighbour   queue   soldier   secretary
> nuisance   definite   leisure   muscle

m	u	s	c	l	e	q	g	g	a	s
a	j	b	w	e	q	g	o	h	j	e
w	d	e	f	i	n	i	t	e	d	c
h	v	h	m	s	x	m	a	z	y	r
c	e	x	n	u	i	s	a	n	c	e
m	f	b	g	r	s	o	n	b	m	t
q	u	e	u	e	h	l	k	p	z	a
y	o	y	g	o	c	d	s	z	e	r
j	s	d	k	f	l	i	f	v	n	y
p	r	i	v	i	l	e	g	e	k	n
x	d	f	k	r	y	r	v	m	c	k
n	e	i	g	h	b	o	u	r	v	e

Spelling <u>nuisance</u> words

Can you remember these spellings? Read the words.
Focus on the tricky parts. Cover the word, write it in the
next column then uncover the word to check the spelling.
Do this again, twice more.

Read the word	Write the word	Write the word	Write the word
soldier			
thorough			
stomach			
shoulder			
secretary			
restaurant			
queue			
privilege			
mischievous			
parliament			
persuade			
neighbour			
nuisance			
definite			
leisure			
muscle			

Enough tough spellings!

Cut out these cards. Match up the words that rhyme.

Note: each pair of words must have one word with an **ough** spelling.

Stick the words down as pairs on another sheet of paper.

Underline the matching vowel in each pair.

sort	tough	brought	through
threw	cuff	fought	although
taught	snow	rough	puff
stuff	bought	enough	though
cough	low	fort	off

Complete these sentences using three of these **ough** words.

tough   brought   through   although   bought   enough   though   cough

1.   Mum _____ me some new shoes.

2.   Have you _____ your coat?

3.   Stop! That's _____ ketchup!

Thoroughly tough words

Read the phonetic versions of these words.
Write the correct spelling of each word.

/coff/ _____

/troff/ _____

/ruff/ _____

/tuff/ _____

/enuff/ _____

/drowt/ _____

/brort/ _____

/nort/ _____

/thort/ _____

/ort/ _____

/bort/ _____

/althoe/ _____

/thoe/ _____

/doenut/ _____

/thura/ _____

/bura/ _____

Write a homophone for each of these words.

ruff _____

threw _____

fort _____

bow _____

Complete these sentences.

1. Toby _____ a new computer game
   with his birthday money.

2. Has everyone _____ in their reply slips?

Sorting 'silent' letters

Read these words and underline the 'silent' letters.

Write the words in the correct column of the table.

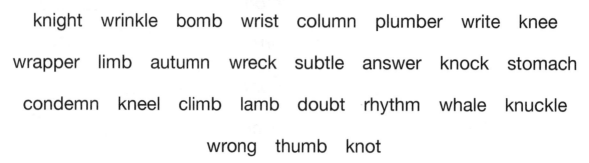

knight   wrinkle   bomb   wrist   column   plumber   write   knee

wrapper   limb   autumn   wreck   subtle   answer   knock   stomach

condemn   kneel   climb   lamb   doubt   rhythm   whale   knuckle

wrong   thumb   knot

'Silent' b	'Silent' n	'Silent' w	'Silent' h	'Silent' k

Subtle spellin

Read th_____ the missing word
f_____

1. _____ rite/

2. _____ range and red.   /ortum/

3. _____ the surprise party.   /suttle/

4. _____ hone please? I'm

5. L_____ _____ of Madagascar.
   /iland/

6. The _____ came to fix the leak.   /plummer/

7. Please _____ your hair before leaving for school.
   /coam/

8. All that was left of the Greek temple was one _____.
   /colum/

9. Is that your _____ rumbling?   /stumack/

10. Don't _____ too high!   /clime/

11. Dance in time to the _____.   /rithm/

12. 'Orca' is another name for a killer _____.   /wale/

13. The boys threw water _____ at each other in the garden.   /boms/

14. The bear caught the _____ as it leapt up the waterfall.   /sammon/

Lightning crossword

Practise spelling some tricky words. Read the clues and carefully write the words in the crossword grid. Use the words at the bottom of the page to help you.

Across

1. Relating to the body

6. Terrible, causing great damage, catastrophic

8. In a sincere way

9. A flash of light in a storm

Down

2. A medium-sized sailing boat

3. A machine used for transportation

4. An area of discoloured skin from being hit

5. An item sold at a better-than-usual price

7. Between eleventh and thirteenth

-------------------------- fold here --------------------------------

vehicle   physical   bargain   sincerely   disastrous   twelfth   lightning   yacht   bruise

Disastrous Snakes and Ladders

Play a game of Snakes and Ladders with a partner.
You will need a counter each and a dice. Start at the
bottom left-hand corner of the board. Roll the dice and move
your counter.

If you land on a ladder, zip to the top of the ladder. Close your eyes and spell the
word you've landed on. If you spell it correctly, you can stay on that word. If not,
return to the last word you were on.

If you land on a snake, slide to the bottom of the snake. Close your eyes and spell
the word you've landed on. If you spell it correctly, you can return to the last word
you were on. If not, you must stay at the bottom of the snake.

If you don't land on a snake or a ladder, close your eyes and spell the word you've
landed on. If you spell it correctly, you can stay on that word. If not, return to the
last word you were on.

The winner is the first to the Finish.

Page 1 of 2

Unit 9B Resource 2

48. accommodate	**49.** occur	**50.** immediately	**Finish**
47. correspond	**46.** attached	**45.** committee	**44.** exaggerate
40. suggest	**41.** recommend	**42.** occupy	**43.** programme
39. necessary	**38.** profession	**37.** immediate	**36.** apparent
32. interrupt	**33.** opportunity	**34.** excellent	**35.** embarrass
31. marvellous	**30.** soldier	**29.** thorough	**28.** stomach
24. parliament	**25.** persuade	**26.** restaurant	**27.** shoulder
23. mischievous	**22.** privilege	**21.** queue	**20.** neighbour
16. muscle	**17.** leisure	**18.** definite	**19.** nuisance
15. bargain	**14.** category	**13.** disastrous	**12.** yacht
8. sincerely	**9.** vehicle	**10.** vegetable	**11.** bruise
7. signature	**6.** awkward	**5.** forty	**4.** lightning
Start	**1.** twelfth	**2.** variety	**3.** physical

A 'conscious' or 'conscience' controversy

Write the missing words in the sentences.

> hindrance   controversy   amateur   system   conscious
>
> unconscious   conscience   desperate

1.   Tom isn't _____ of the world around him when he plays computer games.

2.   Uncle Jim was knocked _____ by the cricket ball.

3.   Peter's _____ pricked him slightly when he ate his sister's biscuit.

4.   Lily's tantrums were a _____ to everyone enjoying the outing.

5.   On Saturday, Ronnie and Sam played in the _____ golf tournament.

6.   There was a dreadful _____ about closure of the sports centre.

7.   Suzy was _____ to go to her best friend's party.

8.   There is a new _____ for paying for dinner at school.

Playing with words

Add the suffix to the root word. Write the word. Remember, you might need to change the spelling of the root word.

1. frequent + ly   _____

2. hinder + ance   _____

3. govern + ment   _____

4. pronounce + ation   _____

5. disaster + ous   _____

6. twelve + th   _____

7. sincere + ly   _____

8. marvel + ous   _____

9. desperate + ly   _____

10. immediate + ly   _____

11. embarrass + ment   _____

12. awkward + ly   _____

13. correspond + ing   _____

14. communicate + tion   _____

Are you <u>weary</u> of spelling mistakes?

Match the words in the box to their meanings.

| affect   weary   proceeds   wary   effect   dessert   precedes   desert |

1. _____ – money raised

2. _____ – a place with little or no life

3. _____ – a result

4. _____ – tired

5. _____ – goes before

6. _____ – to influence

7. _____ – pudding

8. _____ – nervous

Proceed to spell effectively

Use the words in the box to complete the sentences.

> desert   affect   wearily   dessert   wary   proceed
>
> precedes   affected   effect

1. My favourite _____ is chocolate Swiss roll and custard.

2. Too much caffeine will _____ your ability to sleep.

3. It has not rained in the Atacama _____ for many years.

4. Missing a lot of school had a bad _____ on Sam's progress.

5. Although the snake handler said it was safe, Oscar was still _____ of the snake.

6. Jonas _____ plonked himself down on the sofa.

7. "Once you've viewed the exhibits, _____ to the next room," said the guide.

8. "Make sure you know who _____ you in the presentation," said Mr Stevens.

9. It was the last day of term and the excitement _____ the children's concentration.

Put spelling errors in the <u>past</u>

Complete these sentences using **past** or **passed**.
Remember **passed** is always a verb; **past** is never a verb.

1. In the _____ , teachers were allowed to hit children with rulers.

2. Clara _____ the plate to Tara.

3. To get to the cinema, you need to go _____ the shops and then turn right.

4. Led is the _____ tense of to lead.

5. My sister has finally _____ her driving test.

6. "Turn around! You've _____ her house," said Karen.

7. Time _____ so slowly as we waited for Granny to come.

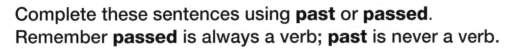

8. It's well _____ your bedtime.

9. I'm _____ caring which film you choose!

10. The moon _____ in front of the sun causing an eclipse.

A full <u>complement</u> of homophones

Look at the words at the bottom of the page. Learn to spell them and remember the meaning of each. Fold back the bottom of the page to hide the words. Use the words to fill the gaps in these sentences.

1. Josh was pleased with the way his new jumper _____ his trousers.

2. The boys made a good _____ from their cake sale.

3. The guide explained the _____ written on the tomb.

4. Jasmine looked in the _____ cupboard for some more paper.

5. Victoria _____ Kat on her new hairstyle.

6. He made such _____ promises, he couldn't keep all of them.

7. Daniel crashed the _____ together with great enthusiasm.

8. The _____ told the dwarves what the future held for them.

9. The traffic in town was _____ and the girls were very late for ballet.

10. I am _____ for the toilet!

- fold here -

complimented   complemented   prophet   profit   stationery   stationary
symbols   cymbals   desperate   disparate

Practising practice and practise

Choose **s** or **c** to complete these sentences.

1.   My dad keeps his driving licen___e in the car.

2.   The theatre licen___ed the music for the show.

3.   It can be hard to listen to advi___e from your parents.

4.   Stefan advi__ed his sister to behave in Mr Logan's class.

5.   Marge had a clever devi___e that fed her cat while she was away.

6.   The professor devi___ed a system to make toast using solar energy.

7.   Practi__e makes perfect.

8.   Hal practi__es the bassoon every morning.

9.   Football practi___e is on Tuesdays and Thursdays.

Higher homophones

Look at the words at the bottom of the page and remember
what each word means. Practise the spelling. Fold back
the bottom of the page to hide the words. Then write the correct
word to complete each sentence.

1. The blocked _____ on my chin is very sore.

2. I'm so _____ – I have nothing to do!

3. Which mountain is _____ : Scafell Pike or Snowdon?

4. The café was a very welcome _____ at the end of the hike.

5. Where can we _____ bats and balls for table tennis?

6. I have spent all my pocket money and now I am very _____ .

7. My trousers are too short and too tight on the _____ .

8. Battle Abbey was built on the _____ of
    the Battle of Hastings.

9. We can nail your model train track to this
    wooden _____ .

10. Please don't _____ the silver paper;
    only take what you need.

- fold here -

hire   higher   site   sight   bored   board   pore   poor   waste   waist

Homophone crossword

Use the words at the bottom of the page to complete this crossword. Watch out: you won't need all the words.

Across

2. A moral standard

5. A small island

7. The first version of a piece of writing

8. Out loud

Down

1. A space between rows of seats

3. A breakfast meal

4. The main thing

6. A story told in many parts

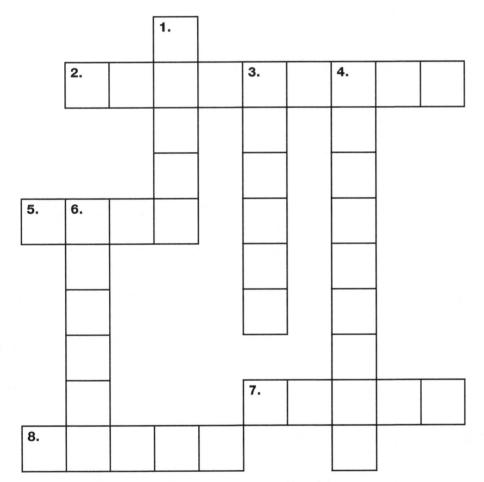

- fold here -

serial   cereal   aisle   isle   aloud   allowed   draught   draft   principal   principle

A short <u>course</u> in more homophones

Use the words in the box to complete the sentences.

bite	byte	caught	court	course	coarse
	currant	current	laps	lapse	

1. The French language _____ ran for ten weeks.

2. The river was full and its _____ was strong and fast.

3. A _____ is a very small piece of information on a computer.

4. The only thing I _____ when fishing was a cold.

5. First, start with the _____ sandpaper, then use the smooth.

6. Don't _____ off more than you can chew.

7. The fitness session started with five _____ of the pitch.

8. Diane bought five _____ buns and two doughnuts.

9. Tim walked onto the tennis _____ feeling rather nervous.

10. Due to a momentary _____ of concentration, we missed the turning.

Who's decent at spelling?

Read the words at the bottom of the page and try to remember them. Fold back the bottom of the page to hide the words. Use the words to complete the sentences. Watch out: you won't need all the words.

1. The house was made with a _____ frame covered in concrete.

2. Hold on to the rope and control your _____ down the tower.

3. I was in _____ for a long time after my cat died.

4. My step- _____ is a kind and _____ man.

5. Does anyone know _____ turn it is to go first?

6. The protesters gathered to voice their _____ about the new road.

7. How much _____ is it to the museum's gift shop?

8. The bride and the _____ party arrived at the wedding reception.

9. Do not _____ to racism or sexism, ever.

10. Grace and Abe crept into the kitchen to _____ a cake.

- fold here -

ascent   assent   descent   dissent   decent   morning   mourning
steal   steel   who's   whose   father   farther   bridal   bridle

Homophones: There's meaning at <u>stake</u>

Read the words at the bottom of the page and try to remember them. Fold back the bottom of the page to hide the words. Use the words to complete the sentences. Watch out: you won't need all the words.

1. It is important to _____ people when they do well.

2. As the footballer goes to take the penalty, half the stadium _____ he misses.

3. Watch as the lion _____ on the smallest member of the herd.

4. Kittens, puppies and ducklings are all so _____!

5. The mist lifted off the mountain and the _____ could be seen at last.

6. Mary stomped off in a fit of _____ when she wasn't picked for the netball team.

7. The queen sits on her hard _____ and longs for a cushion.

8. I wish I hadn't _____ away my old teddy.

9. The film star reserved a whole _____ of rooms at The Ritz.

10. Tie the tomato plant to a _____ when it grows too tall to stand alone.

11. _____ and chips is a perfect combination.

- fold here -

praise   prays   preys   peek   peak   pique   thrown
throne   sweet   suite   stake   steak